S0-AFN-197

Other Works by May McGoldrick,
Nik James & Jan Coffey

NOVELS BY MAY McGOLDRICK

A Midsummer Wedding

The Thistle and the Rose

Angel of Skye (Macpherson Trilogy Book 1)

Heart of Gold (Book 2)

Beauty of the Mist (Book 3)

Macpherson Trilogy (Box Set)

The Intended

Flame

Tess and the Highlander

The Dreamer (Highland Treasure Trilogy Book 1)

The Enchantress (Book 2)

The Firebrand (Book 3)

Highland Treasure Trilogy Box Set

Much Ado About Highlanders (Scottish Relic Trilogy Book 1)

Taming the Highlander (Book 2)

Tempest in the Highlands (Book 3)

Scottish Relic Trilogy Box Set

Arsenic and Old Armor

The Promise (Pennington Family)

The Rebel

Secret Vows Box Set

Borrowed Dreams (Scottish Dream Trilogy Book 1)

Captured Dreams (Book 2)

Dreams of Destiny (Book 3)

Scottish Dream Trilogy Box Set

Romancing the Scot

It Happened in the Highlands

Sweet Home Highland Christmas

Sleepless in Scotland

Dearest Millie

How to Ditch a Duke

Highland Crown (Royal Highlander Series Book 1)

Highland Jewel (Book 2)

Highland Sword (Book 3)

Ghost of the Thames

Thanksgiving in Connecticut

Made in Heaven

Marriage of Minds: Collaborative Writing

Step Write Up: Writing Exercises for 21st Century

NOVELS BY NIK JAMES

Caleb Marlowe Westerns

High Country Justice

Bullets and Silver

Silver Trail Christmas

MARRIAGE OF MINDS

Collaborative Writing

NIKOO MCGOLDRICK
JAMES A. MCGOLDRICK, PH.D.

Best Wishes!
Nikoo & John

MM Books

Copyright © 2021 by Nikoo and James A. McGoldrick

Marriage of Minds: Collaborative Writing

All rights reserved.

The first edition of this book was published by Heinemann, a division of Reed Elsevier, Inc.

No part of this book may be reproduced in any form or by any electronic or mechanical means, including information storage and retrieval systems, without written permission from the author, except for the use of brief quotations in a book review.

Cover Art by Melinda De Ross at CoveredbyMelinda.com

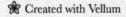 Created with Vellum

To the memory of
Tom Kepple

A giving nature never dies.

Contents

Note on the 2nd Edition

When we originally came up with the idea of *Marriage of Minds* twenty years ago, we wanted to produce a book that would be helpful to writers who were struggling on their own and who thought that collaborating with someone else might be the answer. Since then, we've heard from a multitude of writing teams who have successfully collaborated on novels and works of nonfiction. They all found that our book served as a tremendous aid to their efforts. But the feedback we received also said something more significant:

- Many used *Marriage of Minds* in dealing with and training for conflict management at work.
- Couples used *Marriage of Minds* to understand and improve their relationships.
- *Marriage of Minds* was even spotted on wedding registries.

The two of us live together, work together, play together, spend our life together, 24/7. Needless to say, it was no revelation that what we covered in the book was our accumulated knowledge of everything that goes into making a successful collaboration in life and career. And the encouraging words from readers warmed our hearts.

- No one knows more about collaborative writing than you two. (We're honored ... and flattered.)
- Your honesty and wisdom really comes through. (That's putting *way* too much pressure on us.)
- You've been doing this a long time. (Tell us about it.)
- Write another book on this topic.

Yes, with enough compliments we *can* be pressured. ☺

After much brainstorming and armed with the wealth of knowledge offered by others in our first edition of *Marriage of Minds*, we decided to substantially revise and publish this second edition.

We hope *Marriage of Minds* helps you in your pursuit of whatever you've been searching for in your creative *and* personal life.

Please write to us and share your collaboration experiences. Perhaps we'll include your wisdom in future editions of this work.

Nikoo & Jim McGoldrick
    AKA May McGoldrick, Jan Coffey, and Nik James
    Valentine's Day 2021 (*So* romantic!)

Introduction

When Edgar Allan Poe's sleuth, C. Auguste Dupin, takes on the job of finding the purloined letter in the famous short story, he doesn't turn his antagonist's chambers upside down. Unlike his friend, the eminent Prefect of Police, our hero doesn't pry up the floor boards or drill the legs of the chairs in search of hollowed-out hiding places. He doesn't even look behind a single painting.

He doesn't have to.

The object of the Prefect's search, that stolen letter, is right there in the open, tacked to the fireplace mantle where all can see it.

And overlook it.

In a way, writing and publishing can be like that. How many of us, day in and day out, labor at our craft with blinders on? How many of us – cut off from the world in the little shoe boxes in which we write – fail to recognize what we need to do to write successful stories?

What is it then, that makes one person a Nobel laureate and another a waiter, laboring at the craft of writing for a lifetime of obscurity. What makes one person an "Auguste Dupin" and another a "Prefect of Police."

In another galaxy – not so far away and not so long ago – we were among the ranks of those unpublished writers, laboring long hours at the craft. We, working individually, devoured books on writing, enrolled in classes and workshops, read and wrote and read and wrote.

If only there had been a book like this one.

And then, one winter, something happened. We found the purloined letter.

For the tenth time in a month, ice and snow had coated our trees, our street, our walks, and even our windows. This was the stormiest winter in any of our thirteen years of marriage – both inside and out. Our sensitivity to one another – and our search for ourselves – had developed to a critical point as we continued to deal with highly demanding jobs, our marriage, and our children. We attributed some of this turmoil to the personal aftershocks following the heart surgery of our infant son.

So here we were, snowbound and feeling...what? Some might have called it midlife crisis – but in our thirties? We knew we needed a change. We needed something more.

Well, those standing outside our life and looking in thought so. After all, from their vantage point, we had successful careers, a solid marriage, and a growing family. Change is bad, we could hear them say. If it ain't broke, don't fix it.

But even if it "weren't broke," the wheels were definitely starting to wobble.

We've all had the feeling. That nagging regret that you've never really pursued your dream. That panicky rush when you wake up thinking that you've missed something, and that you might just be too late to find it. It's the Hemingway Syndrome. That feeling you get in an airport that life is too short. If I just get on that plane, we think, in a few hours I could be in Paris, Nairobi, Key West, Tahiti. Then I could take those photographs, paint those canvasses, write that novel...

The snow was still falling. The ice was coating everything.

Our feelings seemed to be recalling those years of childhood and adolescence, those times when we wondered what it is that we want to be when we grow up.

For as long as either of us could remember, we both wanted to be writers.

Six years prior to that winter, Jim had given up a successful career path as a manager in a shipyard. He wanted to pursue his dream of going back to school and getting his Ph.D. in English. He'd done that. I, on the other hand, had been tied into a career of engineering and then management. As a woman advancing successfully in a primarily male profession, I had a lot at stake. At the same time, being a storyteller at heart, I viewed writing as my true calling – as a dream that I would never be allowed to pursue. After all, as far as the world around me was concerned, I was the one with an analytical mind. Also, English was my second language. How could I possibly pursue writing in a language that I didn't speak it fluently until I was in college?

But then, this was the snowiest winter in our thirteen years of marriage. Ice was everywhere, and even the firmest ground had become slippery and treacherous.

Another storm. Another day off. An ad in a writer's magazine for a fiction contest. Two people sit down side by side at a computer keyboard. An afternoon of working and reworking some ideas for a short story.

And that was when our troubles *really* began...

Marriage of Minds provides assistance and advice for that journey into the collaborative writing process.

Despite thirteen years of marriage, when we started to write together, we found ourselves on a "first date" when it came to this new battle of creative wills. Could we make this work? In so many ways, the path we took – a path that would lead us to completing that first prize-winning story, then that first novel, then a second, and so on – has been quite similar to the path one travels in the building of a successful marriage. It is a road filled with the same bumps and curves – a journey requiring sacrifice and self-learning.

We have divided *Marriage of Minds* into two parts. Part I is called "Courtship," since the process of finding the right person and of understanding the requirements of a collaborative relationship has a lot in common with preparing for marriage. From topics on recognizing the need for a writing partner, to actually finding the "write" partner, to understanding the details of the "prenuptial" agreement, Part I of this book takes you through the self-preparation essential for the collaborative venture.

Part II, which we call "Marriage à la Modem," is a real "how-to" for writing together. Set up in chapters that cover the mechanical as well as the spiritual challenges of writing with a partner, this section offers advice and instruction on brainstorming, writing, publishing, and even promotion of your work.

In addition to our own experiences, we've gathered accounts from other writing teams who are currently collaborating or have collaborated in the past. Throughout these pages, we'll try to reveal honestly the mistakes we all have made, the joys we've shared, the secrets we've stumbled upon, and the growth we've achieved at every stage. If you decide to try the route of collaborative writing, we can promise you a most exciting and challenging journey.

In fact, you might even be surprised to find your own purloined letter right before your eyes.

PART I

Courtship: Preparing to Write with a Partner

Sonnet 116
WILLIAM SHAKESPEARE

Let me not to the marriage of true minds
Admit impediments. Love is not love
Which alters when it alteration finds,
Or bends with the remover to remove.
Oh no! It is an ever fixèd mark
That looks on tempests and is never shaken.
It is the star to every wandering bark,
Whose worth's unknown although his height be taken.
Love's not Time's fool, though rosy lips and cheeks
Within his bending sickles compass come.
Love alters not with his brief hours and weeks,
But bears it out even to the edge of doom.
If this be error and upon me proved,
I never writ, nor no man ever loved.

1

The Single Life

OR, "I'M GONNA WRITE ME A BOOK."

TO SEE your name in print. To publish a novel. To have the pleasure of browsing the online retailers or the brick-and-mortar bookstores and pausing before a collection of books that *you* have created.

Sounds pretty good, doesn't it?

Nearly all of us have had that dream. Many of us, however, have pushed aside those thoughts, thinking them frivolous at best. For some of us, it has been a matter of timing and priorities. *As soon as I save some money...Hey, the career has to come first...When the kids start first grade...After they go to college...There are simply not enough hours in the day...*

We did the same thing, but for all of our lives we've been aware – sometimes painfully aware – that we each wanted to be writers. We kept our journals. We jotted down lines of poetry. We periodically added to a file of ideas for stories, screenplays, books. We even pursued the idea of moving to Ireland, figuring if you can't write in a place *that* romantic, where *can* you write?

Where we wanted to go, though, and where we were

actually going, did not appear to be the same thing. Life kept getting in the way.

Sure, a person's development as a writer can be compared to learning to walk – mustering the courage for the first step, building the strength to take the next – but writing is actually a far more self-conscious process than walking. Hey, when you're a year old, it doesn't matter if you fall on your face. As an adult, trying to put a story on paper and get it published, each of us has a bit more at stake.

In a way, writing is more like the courting process. Here are our ideas, our talent, and our efforts, we say to readers and publishers. Accept us or reject us. But it is not just our work that we feel we are putting out there, it is *ourselves*. From the author's end, writing is personal. Just like the courtship process. In fact, we see three distinct stages in our development as writers: The Blind Date, Going Steady, and Married with Children.

The Blind Date: Idea Meets Writer

It didn't happen *every* night, I'll grant him that. But 'regularly' would not be overstating things.

I'd say 2:00 AM was his usual hour. So romantic.

It always started with him taking my hand in his. Then, if I didn't immediately respond, the gentle shake of my shoulder. The quiet whisper.

"Are you awake?"

It occurs to me now, I've never thought to tell him no.

"Tell me," I'd whisper instead.

"What do you think of this idea?"

Then, lying there in the dark, I'd listen to his description of an image, a setting, an action indicating the start of something. That's all it ever took. My brain cells, fully alert now, would crank into high gear. My analytical mind would line up its legion of questions...and he would fall peacefully back to sleep.

And then I would lie there, completely awake, tormented. Every time, it seemed, the potential for a story would grab me. Just like the hundred times before, I would be left unfulfilled, never knowing what was to come next.

I've never regretted a moment's lost sleep, though. I've actually enjoyed the time, reimagining and reshaping Jim's stories in my mind. He would rarely tell me much more than a fragment, but then again, there was rarely anything more than a fragment there. But it was always just enough to entice me to push it further. I simply *had* to find out what lay behind this mysterious island town facing west, behind these messages hidden within paintings, behind this strange congregation of people on the mist-enshrouded beach.

It was during this time that I began to consider our midnight sessions as "blind dates." Gradually, the idea began to coalesce in my mind. Hey, if you fall sleep, I decided, I get to do whatever I want with what you tell me. It made perfect sense to me.

Not that I got any more sleep.

Looking back, I realize I used to be a lot nicer person than I am now. These days, I operate on four hours sleep a night, and Jim knows better than to wake me up (unless he has something else in mind).

It made no difference where we were going or how far. Even the noise level of the kids in the back seat made no difference.

Glancing over at her profile, I would always know she was at it again. I could see the concentration in the stare, the furrowed brow, the frown around the mouth, and – now and then – the flicker of a smile. Sometimes a sadistic smile.

And then she would turn to me and say, "Want to hear it?"

"Go."

She would tell me the story. Not the whole thing start to finish. And never with enough detail to take me through the turning points of the plot. I like plot, but that never seemed to be important. She would just give me a glimpse, what we now call a "high concept" description of what the story might be. Just a one sentence clue. Then a brief description of a central character.

And that would be it. Without another word, Nikoo would sink back into that impenetrable silence of hers, go glassy in the eyes again, and leave me hanging.

Sometimes it would be even less, though. Just an image that she thought could be the start of a story. A footbridge over a brook in a green English park. A Jane Doe thrown out of a car on a highway in Connecticut. A casket in the middle of a deserted Texas highway. And of course there had to be a woman, still alive, in that coffin. Even worse, the woman had to be dressed in century-old costume. What was I supposed to do with that?

I can't tell you how many highway exits I've missed pondering these ideas. Blind dates are tough on a man's concentration.

The kids are grown and gone, but it still happens. And my first response these days is, "How *many* drops of CBD did you take?"

So what *exactly* is a blind date?

A blind date in the writing world is someone with an idea for a story.

This concept is nothing new to writers. We meet potential blind dates all the time – at work, online, at the playground, sitting next to us on the plane, at the family gathering. As soon as they know you're writing, the body posture changes. Your brother-in-law's sister's husband pins you in the corner. He's always hated English, he tells you. It was his worst subject. But he's got an *idea* for a story that is worth six figures at least. (The truth is, if he wants to get anywhere with us, he'd better say seven figures and buy us another drink.) He just needs *someone* to write it down for him.

And he's not alone.

The thing that hurts the most is that the ideas are probably pretty good. After all, think of the variety of experiences that people have, of the places they've been, that we as individuals may never experience or visit. In fact, some of them we purposely avoid.

Not long after we published our first novel, we got our first prison letter. We were shocked. Here was a killer, incarcerated for life (thank God!), writing to *us*, and he wanted us to tell his story.

It was a fascinating letter, eight handwritten pages from a guy who had set fire to his first building at the age of eleven. He had started carrying a gun at the age of fourteen and had killed for the first time at sixteen. The *first* time. This was a man who had been involved with every facet of organized crime in every city from Philadelphia to Boston. A killer who had gone out on furlough from a prison in New England to make a contract hit on another mobster. At the time of sending us the letter, he had two contracts out on him for turning state's evidence.

Now, here's a swell blind date, we tell ourselves. How do we tell him that we don't want to write his story?

We don't want him to love us. We don't want him to hate us. We just want him to take down the newspaper clipping with our picture from his wall.

So we sent a copy of his letter to a nonfiction crime writer we know.

At a recent conference, a gentleman approached us with another proposal. Actually, he came offering to pay us to write his biography. His story, too, fascinated us. A World War II veteran and a fairly successful singer on the nightclub circuit, he had experiences covering over five decades that included some of the most celebrated entertainment personalities of our time.

An incredible life story, so we gave him some ideas.

Though we're not in the market for a writing job like that, we told him, we know that there are lots of people willing to ghostwrite his story for him.

To be honest, our own first stab at collaborative writing was really the result of a blind date. After reading a call for submissions to a story contest, Jim came up with the original concept for a story involving a young man struggling against the forces of a hurricane while sailing in the waters off Newport, Rhode Island. When he came to Nikoo and she expressed her concerns about the idea, a subtle shift occurred in the relationship. Actually, at that moment the shift was not very "subtle." But as the ensuing collaborative literary effort began to emerge, we realized that this dynamic aspect of our relationship was new and different. And as we worked together on the story, the original idea became transformed into something entirely new...entirely better...by the shaping forces of our combined imaginative effort.

That one blind date launched us toward a new stage in our creative and professional lives.

Going Steady: A Writer Makes A Commitment

How many blind dates turn into steady relationships? How many people with ideas actually become writers and turn those ideas into manuscripts?

We could stop right here and give you a page or two of statistics showing how small the number is, but we'd much rather say, DEFY STATISTICS. Collaboration is what enabled *us* to make the commitment and beat the odds. But no matter what the numbers say, *you* are the one who makes the difference. This has nothing to do with talent or luck, only with the decision to write and the effort required to follow through.

No one but you can make that decision. No one but you can follow through on the commitment.

If you write one page a day, in a year you will have a novel.

As simple as this sounds, it's true. Good novel or lousy, you will have a novel, and the only thing you can't revise is a blank page.

Actually, this statement says something else too. Aside from the idea that you are approaching your project with an end in mind, the *page-a-day* concept also indicates that writing can be a habitual activity. So you write, every day, whether the Muse visits or not. As our good friend and novelist Christine Bush puts it,

If you're waiting for inspiration, you're a waiter.
If you're writing every day, you're a writer.

But what about the time constraints, the pressures of *real life*? We all have those pressures, and we all live with them. But how can we squeeze that extra hour out of the twenty-eight hours a day that we already have scheduled for ourselves? Well, this is where — as we will discuss later — the collaborative effort can play an integral part.

For years, while we were writing separately, finding time was perhaps the most difficult challenge in our lives. We thought we were disciplined; we imagined ourselves as writers. But truthfully, when it came right down to it, we usually put anything and everything before our writing, before working at our craft.

When we finally started our creative collaboration, though, our priorities shifted a bit. Working on "the book" became a *real* thing that both of us were putting effort into, and "getting it done" began to assert itself as a *real* need. Before, it seemed we couldn't find the time to spend even an hour a day writing. Now, *together*, we were able to identify more time for writing than we ever thought possible.

We wrote our first three books between the hours of 8 PM and midnight. Now, this was after putting in ten hour days at our day jobs and fitting in whatever volunteer activities were on the calendar. Did something have to give? Yes, we found we were sleeping a little less, exercising only when we took the dog out, and watching no television. The house was a little dustier, and the lawn was looking a bit more ragged than usual. But the pages were accumulating.

Was this a good way of doing it? For us, yes. But again, you have to find your own way.

Of course, one of the reasons this worked for us was because we had a mutual support system built in. Naturally, it's a bit easier having your collaborator living under the same roof, breathing the same air, and feeling the same pressure. But there are drawbacks to that too, which we'll share later. A lot of people tell us they'd probably murder their significant other if they tried to write with them.

So, what if you're going it alone? What other methods can keep you committed and going steady?

As human beings, we are social creatures.

Our need to feel a part of a social group is a great tool for advertisers. When we spend our money, most of us want to feel smart, sexy, healthy, attractive. Sometimes, we want to feel rebellious and individualistic. Of course, we want to feel rebellious and individualistic just like that smart, sexy, healthy, and attractive person in the ad.

Even health clubs and rehab programs base their results on the same premise. We've all seen how it works. Camaraderie. You sweat and groan in an aerobics or Pilates class or during online spin sessions and take those inches off because thirty other people are going through the same agony. You are not alone. Studies prove that working in groups is far more effective than any solitary routine you could possibly set for yourself.

But it is not your solo method that lacks punch; it's the discipline. Working with others provides the discipline.

In writing, the same need for camaraderie, at some level, exists. And one way to find it, on a professional level, is in the writers' groups, local and online.

These groups have a mission – to get you out of your shoebox, just for a short time, and keep you in contact with people who share your dream. As a part of these groups, you get a chance to connect with scores of other writers who not only share the same goals but are struggling with the same challenges.

**If you want to be a writer, you must think of
yourself as a professional.**

So much information is shared between members of
these groups. From the craft of writing to critique sessions
to industry news. Insights into the goals, personnel, and
contracts of the major publishers. Information on such
topics as literary agents, research methods, and self-promo-
tion. All of this is constantly being shared between fellow
writers.

From our own experience, we've found that many
writers have a giving nature. But it's important to keep in
mind that generosity needs to be reciprocated. Someone
helps you, make sure you help back by buying their books,
leaving a review, promoting their work.

And these groups are an excellent place to meet the
'write' partner.

Married With Children: The Published Writer

You've had great ideas rattling in your head for most of
your life. You've become disciplined, working at your craft
with a routine that your friends and family describe as "driven." Your ticket says, "Publication," that golden destina-
tion of destinations, and you peer ahead toward that point
on the horizon. Finally, because of hard work, talent, and a
bit of luck, your train arrives. You publish your novel.

You climb onboard that literary locomotive, and it
leaves the station. You're riding the rails.

And then the realization sinks in. You have been
thinking all along that this was the end of the line, but you
were wrong. That horizon still stretches out ahead of you.
This stop was only a changing station.

For every successful author, publishing that first novel is

only the beginning, and often, it is a rough whistle stop, at that.

The publication of John Grisham's first novel, *A Time to Kill*, met with resounding silence. Stories of his often futile efforts to sell the novel out of the back of his pickup truck are legendary. They say there is a landfill in Oxford, Mississippi, with a treasure throve of somewhat mildewed Grisham first editions. Though John Grisham moved on to become an incredibly successful novelist, his struggles at the time of his first book's publication are similar to so many first-time authors.

The fears and insecurities of the published author are never-ending.

Do I have more than one book in me? What if I can't finish my second book? How do my sales match up to others' books? Can I fool another publisher into buying my next story? Should I independently publish my work? Can I ever make a living at this and give up my day job?

The professional constantly searches for ways to grow.

- I'll write two books a year.
- I'll write in two different genres.
- I'll plan a workshop a month.
- I'll start blogging.
- I've *got* to go to that darned conference on screenwriting.

It's hard work getting published, but sometimes it's harder to keep writing and keep publishing.

But for every proclamation of doom about the industry, there is a success story. We all hear the stories nearly every day. That debut writer who hits the *New York Times* list. The latest, groundbreaking work that garners a Pulitzer Prize for an established writer. That novelist who, after a dozen category romances, writes a mainstream thriller and gets a seven-figure advance *and* a movie deal.

Our attachment to the books we write is very much like our attachment to our children. They are a product of our physical bodies. They are our babies. In fact, we become known in publishing circles by our books as surely as we become known around town as "Cyrus's mom" or "Sam's dad."

Just as we worry about the ones that walk and talk, we worry about the health of our literary "children," and we worry about the future of those "unborn" books that we have yet to produce. We even worry about whether we'll be *able* to produce more interesting, vital offspring. Like Ponce de Leon in search of the Waters of Eternal Youth, we sometimes find ourselves searching for fertility drugs for the imagination.

So how does the concept of collaborative writing play a part in the world of the published author? To come up with interesting stories, to keep that fresh voice, to publish in different genres, and to grow productively in our chosen craft. The published author thinks (or should be thinking) of these things, and collaborative writing *might* offer an answer.

Melissa Scott had been successfully publishing science fiction novels and stories for four years before collaborating on a fantasy novel with Lisa Barnett. In 1987, the two women became attracted to the idea for a story involving an alternate history set in 16th century England. Though previously published, Scott immediately saw advantages to collaborating with Barnett:

> When we started working together, I knew Lisa wrote better dialogue than I did, and – since the book was set in Elizabethan England, a period that *required* good, even brilliant, dialogue – I knew that was going to be a huge help. She is also drawn to different kinds of characters than I am (her lead character in *The Armor of Light* was Sir Philip Sidney, mine was Christopher Marlowe, which about sums up the difference), and over time that's been a huge contribution. She's forced me to tell different kinds of stories, about different kinds of people.

We've found that there are many writers who, in addition to writing on their own, collaborate at some level with other writers. A number of bestselling authors we know get together periodically to brainstorm plots for future books. Evan and Anne Maxwell, a husband and wife team, write separately under the name of Evan Maxwell and Elizabeth Lowell. Together, they write under the name of Ann Maxwell. Talented, creative, and prolific. This collaborative team is all of this and more.

So again, publishing that first book is not the end of all travail. That "happily ever after" does not mean the wedding, by any means. Getting to the altar might be fun, but that next stage – married with children – offers unique challenges and joys, as well.

"Matchmaker, Matchmaker...": The Business Of Publishing

Writers, at any stage of their career, might one day perceive themselves as cast members eyeing the last lifeboat in a deck scene from *Titanic*. Our "competitors" are everywhere, all around us, all vying for that precious seat. Writers of all ages and types, all with that look in their eyes. And we all know how cold the water is.

Yes, indeed...*publish or perish!*

It has always been the case that finding a traditional publisher is difficult and competitive. Nothing has changed. There are many talented people out there, hungry to be published. Just like you.

What *has* changed is that the opportunity for publishing your own work has never been easier. Once writers have a story – written and revised and polished – everything that is needed to put that book in front of a reader is available. Book formatting programs are accessible and easy to use. Platforms for publishing and selling your books in ebook or print or audio are now available to you. Marketing and publicity firms and workshops for do-it-yourselfers are online and waiting to help writers with that business aspect of the industry.

Publishers, however, still need stories to print and sell. They *want* fresh voices and new talent. Literary agents, traditionally the real "matchmakers" in the industry, don't (or at least shouldn't) make any money unless they can successfully introduce a talented storyteller to a publisher and help that relationship grow and bear fruit. None of that has gone away, if that's the route you choose.

Bottom line, writers are empowered like never before.

Focus on what you *can* control.

What if…
What if…
What if…
There are a million 'what ifs' in life. But what good is it

to worry about things you *can't* control? How can the creative side of your brain function when the other side is moaning and groaning?

We recommend that you keep your focus on more productive mental activity.

Keep a journal of your own "blind date" ideas.

One of the questions most often asked during our workshops is, "Aren't you afraid of running out of ideas?" Our answer is always NO.

First of all, because there are two of us, running short on story ideas is never a problem. Collaborative brain-storming – one idea triggering another – produces a plethora of story concepts that we record and keep for the future.

In the years before publishing our first book, we took notes on dreams and collected travel brochures. We had a notebook for ideas. We cut articles out of the newspaper and, most importantly, woke each other up in the middle of the night to share our ideas and plots and premises. Happily, we can say that we still use many of those same techniques, even if we have added online resources like Pinterest as a place to store our research and ideas.

Finding a method of documenting your ideas is an important step in starting to write *the book*. Notebooks, index cards, files, shoeboxes with odds-and-ends – Pinterest – it's really up to you. Whatever method or methods you choose, the key element is that you are ready for that moment when an idea emerges from the mist.

We have found that the thing we call "The Notebook" has remained one of our most essential writing tools. Orig-inally, it functioned as a prewriting research repository and a daily record-keeping device for "Words Written." It now serves as an individual project record where we plan scenes and flesh out plots and create character backstories. Even though we currently keep our lists of characters and daily word count on spreadsheets, each story's spiral notebook provides a central "location" for everything pertaining to a project – beyond the actual text that we're writing.

Having it keeps us prepared for the moment when we do nothing else but write.

Make writing a habit.

This is another thing you can control. You say that you're not prepared to "go steady." There is nothing wrong with that. But you have to start somewhere. Anywhere. Write emails to a friend. Start a blog. Keep a daily journal on how you spend your time. On how your neighbor spends his time...but tread carefully there. Write a poem about your dog. Write a poem *to* your dog...tread *very* carefully there. Spend fifteen minutes in front of the computer and stare at the screen, but don't get down on yourself if you blink before the monitor does.

Instead of staring into space, write something. Anything. In fact, with regard to what you write, we're going to let you off the hook here. Listen carefully:

You can make mistakes, and it will not be a waste of time.

You don't have to write a prizewinning first draft. You don't even have to worry about grammar and punctuation yet.

At this point in the game, your goal is to work on discipline. Fifteen minutes a day this week might turn quite painlessly into half an hour a day next week. Or an hour the week after. No matter what the length of time, your goal is to make writing a habit. An *enjoyable* habit. Face it, it's rewarding to see the words and ideas accumulate. It's gratifying to see characters begin to take shape.

And *don't* keep reworking the first few pages. Push ahead. Keep going.

Now say the words. Admit to your level of commitment. You're "going steady."

You write every day; therefore, you are a writer. You have time and talent invested. You have a professional attitude about yourself and your goals.

Now, don't blow it. Don't set yourself up for disappointment by endlessly guessing at the size of your first advance, or by daydreaming over the keyboard about Steven Spielberg and James Cameron, who are both, of course, waiting breathlessly to buy the movie rights.

I dream of the Academy Awards all the time. Every time, I have a different acceptance speech.

One night, I'll be trying a humor angle and find no one laughing at my jokes. Another night, I'll be pulling a Cuba Gooding, Jr., thanking every person I ever met in my life and finding myself carried off the stage. Another night, a political statement. Another, humility. Whatever the scenario, I always wake up sweating, glad that it was only a dream.

I'm pumped up in the morning, though, and ready to keep working on that next bestseller.

It's brutal, trying to fit an entire guest spot on *The View* into a single shower. But I often try anyway. Sometimes, I'm sweet and just answer the questions that they ask.

Other times, I get riled up and let an interviewer from the *East Bumble Tribune* (or *The New York Times*) have it both barrels for not showing proper respect for woman's fiction. However the imaginary interviews go, they invariably last longer than the hot water.

After that, I'm always ready to face the challenges of finishing that novel. Who wouldn't be?

Of course, we all dream. We wouldn't be writers if we didn't. There is nothing wrong with dreaming, so long as you don't let the dreaming keep you from working. Find the balance. Remember the old saying – a person gazing at the stars is forever at the mercy of the puddles in the road. True enough, but only if the writer is walking alone.

If you get stuck, take inventory of your skills.

Identifying your own strengths and weaknesses is a key element in this writer's journey. Now more than ever, perhaps, in order to convince an agent to represent you, or to entice a publisher to look at your work (if that's the path you decide to go), you need to have an excellent query letter; a clear, engaging synopsis; and a well-crafted, professional looking manuscript. Can you produce those things?

Of course, that spellbinding story of yours is essential. But at this point in your career, you are the seller and they are the customer. You are not yet partners. We can't tell you how many times we've heard editors and literary agents say that their approach to those unsolicited manuscripts is often a process of elimination. If talent and professionalism do not leap off of page one, then there might not be a page two.

You have made the commitment of your time and your talent, though. There is nothing you can't do.

Armed with an inventory of your strengths and weaknesses ("I need to find a better balance of dialogue and narrative," or "My secondary characters are just stereotypes."), now take the time to work on the *craft* of writing. Attend workshops. Go to conferences. Take classes. Join a critique group. Read self-help books. Get involved with writers' communities.

Search for a collaborator.

All along, continue to write. Many talented writers lose sight of their goal at this stage. It's easy to get lost in the detail and forget the reason why you started the journey in the first place. Wasn't it just to tell a good story?

Another thing. Perfection is good. Networking is invaluable. But you must remember that there *is* a moment when a manuscript is ready to submit…or to be published independently.

Your work will never be published if it's lost in computer folder or sitting in a drawer.

As you get close to finishing or revising your manuscript, set a deadline for yourself, polish the thing, and get it out there.

Once published, accept the responsibilities that come along with being "married with children."

Let's jump forward for a moment and imagine that your first book has been published. Your baby is in the bookstores and online. Or maybe it's your second book. Or your tenth. All the uncertainties that go with writing will continue to gnaw away at your creative energy. The nebulous release date of the next book. Those lukewarm sales figures of the current book. The feeling that you really don't know what your editor wants. That new contract that seems to be taking forever to hammer out. Not enough reviews. Where are the readers? Does anybody want me?

Oh, and then there's the annoying little concern that you don't know where the story you're working on is going.

These worries always seem to be lurking right around the corner, don't they?

Fear not.

Remind yourself that you've done it once, and you can do it again. And as you work at it, try to give back something of what others might have given to *you* at one time or another (even if it was only your sixth-grade teacher who said you have "some" talent as a writer). Give workshops and share your experiences, and build your readership. It's amazing how fast a person's self-esteem can be restored. You're an author; that automatically elevates you in most people's eyes. Don't laugh. It's true.

If you have to start all over again – in a new genre, with a new publisher or a new partner or even a new pseudonym – do it. You know the process. You've walked the walk. And this is worth saying again:

Focus on what you can control.

Whether you're published or not yet published, there is one thing that you *can* control. Your work.

Accept the responsibility of being a writer. Accept the fact that sometimes you are going to feel as if you're on the

Titanic. Accept the fact that you will occasionally be immersed in that cold ocean of anxiety.

Just remember that there were boatloads of survivors from the *Titanic*.

Keep writing.

2

In Search of Mr. or Ms. Write
OR, FINDING THE PERFECT PARTNER

WRITING IS A JOB. Marriage is sacred. Keep the two separate.

This is the advice that we are forever giving potential collaborators who attend our workshops. In so many words, we are telling them,

DON'T even consider writing with your significant other unless you are able to practice "double vision."

What Is Double Vision?

Jim, you have too much action in the plot and no meat in the relationships. That scene is way too violent; you've got more severed heads rolling around than you've got people. That middle paragraph puts me to sleep. No. No. No. A woman would NEVER say that. How could you possibly think...

Oh, honey, it's Tuesday. Could you put the trash barrels out?

Nikoo, this is boring. These two people have been talking for twenty pages straight. There is NOTHING going on here. Have them *do* something. Now, that guy in your scene? Right now, he would be thinking of one thing only. And trust me, it's *not* the fate of Scotland.

Oh, sweetheart, are you taking the dog for a walk?

As creative people, we put ourselves out there for criticism every time we write. Despite the façade of toughness that we might erect around us, we are all jello underneath. There are authors we know who would rather stick needles in their eyes than have their manuscripts read by anyone (other than their editors) before publication. And there are others who feel real anger about revision suggestions they receive *from* their editors.

So, imagine the complications that can arise when you juxtapose the creative dynamic with the marital dynamic. Worlds can collide, and it's not always pretty.

It's a lot easier to deal with your anger, hurt, and disappointment when you're not married to, or living with, your writing partner. You don't have to face them across the dinner table. After all, there are enough normal pressures in every family. There are expectations in every relationship. In the ones that endure, there is real personal investment.

It is very difficult to separate the personal and the professional.

Of course, these feelings are not a prerequisite to the

collaboration process. For a first timer though, one who has not been down this specific path before, it's quite easy to stumble into the potholes.

Working with your significant other requires that double vision we mentioned, that ability to see your partner as a creative professional as well as the person who mows the lawn or cooks the meals. As professional writers, you need to have the ability to flip a switch, shift gears – not only with regard to your daily routines, but with your emotions, as well.

Stay calm, she's being critical of the scene, not of me.
So he doesn't like the chapter ending. I won't pout.

Many will tell you that this is easier said than done. Life is hard enough on a relationship as it is. Do you really want to drop a tornado like creative collaboration onto the family farm?

We did, and we have a better relationship because of it.

In Part II of this book, we'll get further into the "how-to" of collaborative writing, with some specifics about how to write with that other person, whether he or she is your significant other, your spouse, your sister, your cousin, your friend, or the stranger that you just hooked up with on the Internet. The one who *seems* to have just the right stuff for collaboration.

First, though, we need to find you the 'write' partner.

The Search

It may seem very natural to choose as your writing partner that friend of yours who has been there for you since first grade. You might even be shocked to find that your next door neighbor has been working at writing for years. Now, that's convenient. Think for a moment, however, about what will happen if the collaboration *doesn't* work out. Are you willing to break a lifelong friendship simply because you jumped into this venture too quickly? Do you have it in your budget to erect a seventy foot long, electrified chain link fence between your neighbor's house and yours because of a disagreement over plot?

Before you decide on a writing partner to collaborate with, it's critical that you do *the search*.

Friends. Significant others. Critique partners. Members of professional organizations you belong to. Everywhere you look, there are potential collaborators.

These days, with the ease of communication provided by social media, there are more ways of finding a collaborator (and collaborating) than ever before.

In Appendix A, we've included a sample list of resources available to a writer in search of a partner. A disclaimer, though. When we wrote the first edition of this book, we were in the early days of the Internet. By the time this book is in your hands or on your screen, there will probably be many more "links" to pursue. In addition, this list only includes national organizations. It does not include either regional organizations (of which there are *many*) or the growing number of colleges and universities that have creative writing websites.

There are many partnerships that don't succeed in business. In friendship, we relate to one another in ways that are not always consistent with how we must relate to a partner in business. Neighborhoods can get ugly and friendships can be severed just because the collaborating parties were not compatible for this type of venture.

Okay, then how should you decide on compatibility with a potential writing partner? To start with, you must *look at yourself as objectively as you can.*

Can you think of any circumstances or events in your personal history that are helpful in defining yourself as a worker or as a writer? In other words,

Identify your own style.

I had just turned twelve when the tragedy occurred. My classmate, my confidante, my best friend died in a hit-and-run accident one afternoon. All she did was chase a ball into the street. Torn between the anguish of the loss and the need to express my grief somehow, I turned to writing. I sat down and drafted a short story. I poured my heart and soul into those words.

The story dealt with an orphan boy, about my age, who is given a caged bird as a gift by a stranger on a bus. Bringing the gift home, he is faced with the anger of a jealous older sister who complains that she will end up having to take care of the creature. During the verbal argument that follows, the bird escapes the cage. The boy, chasing after it, is hit by a car and dies.

Sad? I thought it was. But to my adolescent mind, the story was filled with all kinds of images of kindness and generosity and freedom that I thought were important facets of how we view and deal with life...and death.

I read my work in my literature class at school, and the story was met with great enthusiasm by my classmates. Full of myself, I brought the work home and read it to my mother.

Her reaction was a bit different. She took me to counseling.

Hurt may not be the best word to describe my feelings at the time. I did, however, lose enthusiasm for an audience.

It was then that I started a diary that turned to a regular journal of ideas, feelings, and even stories. My writing became something very private, in spite of the growing volume of work. I valued the satisfaction that the written words gave me, but at the same time I cared very little about polish or perfection. After all, this was all for my eyes only.

I guess this is still my style. I always have ideas floating in my head, and I have the ability to put them down on the paper at a pretty good rate. Now, as far as revision and fine tuning and finish, well...

———————

One late summer night, my older brother (who was probably around eleven years old at the time) entertained the entire family with a poem he'd written about his throne and his throne room. The throne room was tiled, with a big mirror, and a tub. I must have been going into second grade, and I remember lying in bed and listening to the laughter floating up the stairs.

Wow! They were really having fun, and I wanted to be a part of it. So I decided that I'd write a poem too. But what could I write about?

I remember looking out the window into the dusk at the utility poles on the street. They looked like crosses.

So I wrote my poem. Serious and religious as only a seven-year-old can write serious and religious. Did I mention that it was serious?

The response was...well, polite.

Very nice, they said, exchanging looks with each other. Time for bed, Jim.

Although I was disappointed with the response, I continued to write poems. But most of the time, I just wrote for myself.

I like poetry. I like the conciseness. I like the impact. I like the finish.

All these years later, that's still my style, I suppose. I like coming up with stories and characters. But even more, I like the feel of language. I like imagery that conveys meaning. I like structure. I like revising work to look stylish, finished.

————————

Nikoo provides imagination and story; Jim provides action and description.

Of course, our writing functions are not so cut and dried. We both talk through story ideas, character development, and plot structure. We both involve ourselves with revision and style.

Each has strengths and task preferences, however, and they seem to complement our partner's strengths and preferences. We're compatible.

We'd like you to take a little "compatibility" quiz that we've made up to help you with the search for the perfect partner.

To prepare, look back at any piece of writing that you've done. Go back as many years as you want. The purpose of this is not to depress you or to pump up your ego. We simply want you to look as honestly as possible at yourself *as a writer*.

The Compatibility Quiz

What are your strengths? What are your weaknesses? After each term or phrase, rate yourself on scale of 1 to 10 (1=totally deficient; 5=satisfactorily capable; 10=extremely capable). We'll help you out with scoring the first one, just to get you started.

Generating Ideas

The creative mind generates plots and characters that are different. It finds ways of injecting immediacy into themes that are universal. Love is blind. Money is the root of all evil.

You are one of those people with a constant surge of ideas. When you browse social media or watch the news or spy on people in a mall, you often ask, *what if?* (You are a 10)

You always wanted to write the story of *your* life. You have the ability to come up with a premise for a story but have difficulty thinking beyond that. (You are about a 5)

Every idea you come up with sounds like *Jane Eyre* or the last movie you saw. Or, you are just biding your time, waiting for that great idea to bowl you over. (Don't kick yourself, but give yourself a 1)

Score_____

Inventing and Developing Characters

There is a saying that "great short stories are about events; great novels are about characters." To arouse our interest or concern or compassion, characters must have something in them that we recognize in ourselves – fear, love, envy, self-doubt, aspirations. Circumstances illuminate characters' flaws, but also transform those characters, for better or worse.

Is it easy for you to create these fictional people? Do you know what they look like? Do you know their past, present, and future? Do you feel their pain, their motivation, their aspirations? Do your characters talk back to you? (If you answered yes to the last question, you may need a therapist, not a writing partner.)

Score_____

Creating Conflict

Conflict is the force that pushes back at a character as he or she attempts to reach a goal. Sometimes the conflict is internal. For example, fear of heights might keep a policeman from going up a bell tower after a sniper. Sometimes the conflict is external, such as when one character wants to restore a historic building while another wants to level it for a commercial enterprise.

Do your characters have identifiable internal and external conflicts? Is the conflict between them more than a mere misunderstanding that can be resolved by simply talking it out? Will the resolution of their internal conflict directly enable them to resolve their external conflict?

Score_____

Plotting

How is a plot different from a story?

A story is a sequence of events told in a chronological order. We hear stories every day. A couple wins the lottery. A boy goes to war. A dolphin saves a drowning swimmer. A plot differs from a story in the fact that it sequences events using *causality* as a determining factor. For example, "a man hunts a white whale" is a story, whereas "a man hunts a white whale for revenge" is a plot.

In general, a plot has an introductory section in which a central problem is suggested; a middle section in which the story develops; and a final section in which two essential elements are found – a climax where the central problem is resolved and a denouement where the loose ends are tied up.

Do you like creating detailed plots? Are you familiar with plotting techniques? Do you have the ability to see a beginning, middle, and end to your story before you begin to write? Do you have enough key points of action built into your novel to keep the reader turning the pages?

Score_____

Creating Subplots

A subplot is a secondary story that the novelist threads into the main plot to give more dimension to the central story or to reveal something about a character. In a historical romance, the main plot might involve the historical events (i.e., saving an infant king from foreign invaders), while a subplot might involve an element of the romance (i.e., the heroine's past relationship with the leader of the invaders).

A subplot might also reveal a theme important to the overall story. For example, a subplot involving a character's selfless efforts to create an industry in a poverty-stricken area might reveal something about the need for self-sacrifice in the actions of leaders.

As with plot, are you able to see a beginning, middle, and end in your subplots? Do you have the ability to weave subplots effectively into your story?

Score_____

Dialogue

Dialogue is an essential tool in the novelist's craft. Dialogue helps to define a character. It provides a source of direct interaction and conflict between characters. In many ways, it is the place where most action in a novel takes place, because it is where information is conveyed between characters, requiring verbal or physical response.

How effective are you in writing dialogue? Are you able to create different voices for the different characters in your novel? Can you capture diverse feelings or attitudes in the course of a conversation?

Score_____

Description

Dialogue without description is a screenplay. Setting – but action, as well – must be described clearly, and in a manner that propels the story forward. In Charles Dickens's *Bleak House*, for example, the author's vivid description of a London slum and its suffering inhabitants fiercely influences our perception, in a following scene, of a country estate and the haughty, self-centered aristocrats living there.

Can you use descriptive language to effectively depict what you have personally experienced? Can you effectively describe what you have researched but never seen (as in historical fiction)? Can you effectively conjure the language to describe what you have never seen or what may not even exist (as in fantasy, futuristic, or science fiction novels)?

Score_____

Using Point of View

When the reader is privy to the thoughts and impressions of a given character, then the scene is being told from *that* character's point of view. While Jane Austen's novels are told from a single point of view, Tolstoy's *War and Peace* moves from one character's perspective to the next, thereby providing the reader with a variety of insights.

Can you effectively maintain a single point of view for an extended passage? Have you *intentionally* given the dog, the cat, and the rocking chair a point of view? Do you have a preference (or an obsession) with writing from single versus multiple points of view? (Note – this is an important point to discuss with a potential writing partner.)

Score_____

Ending Chapters

Chapter endings provide a crucial opportunity for writers to propel the reader into the next chapter. Readers can be shocked or left questioning their own understanding of the action. Expectation is thus created that must be gratified. Delaying that gratification until the optimal moment is the novelist's goal.

Do you know when to end a chapter? Does your ending include an element of surprise or misunderstanding or mystery that will encourage a reader to turn the page (rather than put down the book)? Do you use subplots to delay the reader's gratification of expectation?

Score_____

Revision

Writing is revising. John Steinbeck supposedly wrote *Grapes of Wrath* start to finish, virtually without revision, but that was an inspired creation unrepeatable even in his own writing career. Ernest Hemingway, on the other hand, wrote and revised the ending of *A Farewell to Arms* fifty-two times, even getting suggestions from friends like F. Scott Fitzgerald. The rest of us fall somewhere between these two extremes, depending on the amount of planning and "pre-writing" we do before we begin creating the text of our story.

> Do you write a first draft with revision in mind? Do you see revision as a positive part of the writing process? Are you detached and objective about your writing? Do you have the ability to look critically at your own work? Are you willing to throw away large sections of your work in the revision process?

Score_____

Editing

While revision could mean cutting and rethinking entire sections of your novel, editing is the last fine tuning of the manuscript – formatting pages or checking for punctuation, spelling, and word choice errors.

> Does the time-consuming, detailed process of "finish work" give you great satisfaction? Is grammar prominent in your repertoire of writer's skills? Can you punctuate effectively (as opposed to being guilty of "comma abuse")?

Score_____

Doing Research

Even if you decide to write about something you know extremely well, there is still a degree of research required in everyone's writing. Books, travel, interviews, and the Internet all provide essential materials for the writer. The writer must consciously decide, however, how much research is enough and how much of that information should be put into the novel.

Do you have a good sense of balance regarding the mix of fact and fiction? Do you have the discipline to set a deadline on the amount of research in your preparation to write? Do you have a good network and understanding of available resources?

Score_____

Writing Habits...Discipline

Discipline means setting a routine for yourself and sticking by it, even if it is sunny out for the first time in two weeks and a friend comes by with a picnic basket. It means holding to your personal commitment to write during your allotted writing time, whether the Muse decides to visit or not.

Are you a goal setter? Are you driven to achieve those goals? Do you need positive incentives to motivate you?

Score_____

Taking Criticism

We all can take honest, objective criticism, as long as the critic honestly, objectively sees only sheer genius in what we have written. And God help the poor soul if there is anything said that is considered negative. Most of us see the words we write as an extension of ourselves, but really our short story or our novel is a product of our imagination, translated into prose only as skillfully as we can muster on any given day.

> Do you refuse to pout, sulk, or kick the dog because of something your critique partner pointed out about your work? Can you separate yourself from your work and take a positive approach to criticism that is being offered objectively? Can you separate the person (the critique partner) from the comments and forgive them some time in the next century? Do you revel in retaliation?

Score_____

The Business of Writing

There is a creative side of writing, and there is a business side. You can write the finest, most original story ever conceived, but if you don't pursue publishing that masterpiece, it might as well have never been written. Professionals constantly seek to understand as much as they can about their business, from market trends to contracts to promotional requirements. In fact, some writers spend as much time on the business side of publishing as they do on their writing.

> Are you able to put as much energy into the business aspects of your work as the creative aspects? Are you confident in your knowledge and skills in both areas? Can you (once again) separate yourself from your creative efforts and see your writing as a "product"?

Score_____

You have finished the quiz and have rated yourself as objectively as possible on the listed items. The next step is to have your potential partner take the quiz.

There is no passing or failing involved in what you two have already done. But here comes the most critical step in the process – the communication, the matching up of each answer, and the beginning of a professional dialogue.

Do you have the same strengths? The same weaknesses? Do you both like to write description, while neither of you likes to write dialogue? In other words, will you be *complementing* one another, or *competing* with one another? Will there be a glaring deficiency in the work you do together because it is a weakness you *both* have?

Also, most important. Do you agree with one another's responses?

We have found this kind of "matching up" to be so useful in our division of labor. Nikoo, who loves to write dialogue, hates to write synopses. Jim, who likes to polish and add to dialogue, loves the definition and concreteness of writing clear, engaging synopses.

What the above quiz offers is an initial survey of your compatibility with a potential partner. This, however, is only the first step in a *process*, in an ever-*evolving* process. When you re-evaluate your talents and your skills and your preferences after a month of working together – or after a year – you may find that your answers have changed.

In our collaborative writing career, which has spanned decades, we've taken and retaken an inventory of our skill sets again and again. And each time, we've seen a shift in preferences and in skills.

As writers, we learn and grow and develop. With that growth, as our confidence and our knowledge advances, we find ourselves able to take on new roles and new challenges.

But none of this can happen until you complete *the search*.

3

Getting Serious
OR, PREPARING TO TAKE THE LEAP

IN THE BEGINNING of the film *Shakespeare in Love*, the young playwright has work lined up in front of him. He has a play to write. He has money ... well, he has a little money. He has the talent. He has an ear for language. He has the words.

What he doesn't have is his *Muse*.

As he searches for inspiration for the story he is to write, he continues to research, to practice, to listen. In short, he continues to prepare.

It is very interesting that Marc Norman and Tom Stoppard, in *collaborating* on this work, decided to include Christopher Marlowe, perhaps the leading playwright in Elizabethan England. For Will Shakespeare, Marlowe serves as a writer to emulate and to compete with. And he even serves as a collaborator, of sorts, providing Shakespeare with an exotic setting and characters and even solid plot ideas filled with conflict.

And because Will Shakespeare is prepared in his craft, he can move forward with the story as it unfolds in his imagination.

Collaboration. It's been a part of storytelling for as long as storytellers have put their heads together over a campfire or put a quill to parchment. It only makes sense. We all have strengths and weaknesses in our ability to tell a story. Some of us are strong plotters but know deep in our ink stained hearts that having a partner who can add snappy dialogue would improve the story tremendously.

A collaborator. In principal, we might already be sold on the idea. Writing with a partner could be the ticket to literary stardom. But before we delve into this venture, like Shakespeare, we must prepare ourselves individually to be the best writer we can be. And there are steps we can take, we *must* take, to enhance our writing abilities, our own contribution to the production of the story.

Lynne Snead and Joyce Wycoff spell it out for us:

> In a creative collaboration, there is shared responsibility, a co-creation of the project design and expected results, a give-and-take that enhances and builds beyond the original vision.

What we have to give must be the best we can contribute. Unless you are in search of a ghostwriter to transcribe your story onto paper, collaboration is a "give-and-take" venture, one that requires two bodies and minds, willing and ready to overcome whatever challenge lies ahead. We need to work hard. That is our responsibility. We've already taken stock of our talent and our skills. Now we need to be sure that we are continuing to sharpen those abilities for the collaborative effort.

We need to be preparing. We need to be working on our craft.

Take creative writing classes.

Bernice Picard, as an aspiring mystery and science fiction author, started collaborating when her husband enrolled her in a writing class.

A writing class may seem to many of us to be a somewhat daunting proposition. We might tell ourselves that the *kind* of writers that we might run into are not the *kind* of writer we want to be. We might say that the writing class will just be filled with a bunch of kids, and we'll feel out of place. Who knows, the professor might yell at us for our grammar errors.

Well, the truth is that reading and writing and getting honest feedback are the best ways to improve our craft, as scary as that seems. Marcia Thornton Jones, who collaborates with Debbie Dadey on *The Bailey School Kids* stories, a popular children's series, "began to conquer her fear of writing while taking a graduate class at Georgetown College with a professor who had a reputation as very demanding."

Join professional writers' groups.

Professional writers' groups provide a wide range of opportunities and services for the inexperienced and experienced writer. Many of these organizations offer workshops and classes on subjects ranging from writing queries and synopses to crafting plots and characters, and just about anything else the writer might need, including opportunities and information on how to cross the publication line. We've included a list of these organizations in Appendix A.

In addition to craft and business information, joining

these groups means networking and possibly meeting potential collaborators.

David Nickle, a journalist and multi-published author, wrote to us about the start of his first collaborative venture:

> It was a pure lark. The two of us belonged to the same writer's workshop and had just finished critiquing a Santa Claus story that didn't quite do it for either of us. We started to discuss the kind of Santa Claus story we'd like to see − sort of a Mervyn Peak meets Metallica kind of Christmas story, and figured we had nothing to lose trying to write the thing together.

As David found, in the course of working on his own craft, he'd stumbled on a kindred spirit and discovered the collaborative process quite by accident.

Attend writer's conferences and retreats.

The difference between attending these and joining professional organizations is that many conferences and retreats are for a short duration and do not require membership in a sponsoring organization.

Ten years before we ever considered writing together, we attended a weekend conference at Brown University on publishing. There, we met senior editors from major publishing houses and other writers from the area. That experience demystified the entire process of publishing for us. Years later, when we were finally ready to commit ourselves to writing, we had a much clearer understanding of how to proceed.

Relationships 101: A Communications Seminar

William Wordsworth and Samuel Taylor Coleridge, the great poets who collaborated to shape and define the British Romantic period, sometimes had difficulty communicating.

Coleridge, who was prone to speak at great length on almost any subject that struck him, was visited one day by Wordsworth and another gentleman. Coleridge spoke eloquently and without interruption for over two hours, during which time Wordsworth listened gravely and attentively, nodding occasionally as if in agreement.

When the two visitors later left the house, the gentleman turned to Wordsworth, saying that, for the life of him, he could not make head nor tail of Coleridge's speech.

"Did you," he asked the great poet, "understand it?"

"Not one syllable," Wordsworth replied.

Communicating effectively with our partner is the foundation upon which successful collaboration is based. Now that we have determined that we will continue to polish our writing craft skills, we need to work on our interpersonal skills.

But do we know the potential problems and pitfalls?

Ferdinand Fournies, an expert on management in the workplace, refers to one:

The mind thinks at least six times faster than we can speak, and because the mind thinks so much faster, its primary function is a *reactive function*. Of course, the mind receives the information transmitted, but the information is received so fast that the mind reacts even before the message is completed.

As a part of a workshop that we give on collaboration, we often have two participants sit with their backs to each other. While one tries to describe a geometric pattern, the other – in almost every case – cannot wait for the complete set of instructions, and instead races ahead, speculating on what the outcome will be and then trying to see if the instructions that follow support their assumptions.

This is natural. After all, we are all creative thinkers, and we cannot put our creativity on hold. When a partner begins to explain a shape, an image, or a character, the listener cannot tell his or her imagination to wait. No, the predictions that the listener makes about the image is limited only by the parameters that the speaker creates. It is only through the give-and-take of questions and answers that the image becomes more and more ordered. More coherent.

It is through clear communication that the image subtly evolves, eventually becoming the creation of both speaker and listener.

Even the most basic courses in writing tell us to be aware of our audience. How do we perceive the *receiver* of our message? Sometimes we even create a general picture of our audience – their gender, their cultural background, their age, etc..

In communicating with a writing partner, we have a real life person in front of us. We don't have to create any general image of an audience. We have a human being with feelings and insecurities and aspirations to deal with.

First of all, a lot can go wrong if we are not on the same wavelength. Edmund Wilson, the noted critic and writer, tried to collaborate with another successful novelist, Edwin O'Connor, and later wrote of the problems that resulted from the faulty communication of clear goals between the collaborators.

In writing alternate chapters with Ed, I very soon ran into difficulties. He would not always accept my cues or my methods, and I found my narrative blocked. I suspected that this was deliberate and that we were playing a game of chess, and this suspicion has been corroborated by Mrs. O'Connor's telling me that, in sending back Chapter 4, Ed had said to her with satisfaction, "Well, I guess I've got him now."

In this 'partnership,' competition replaced collaboration, and the overall goal of producing a viable story was lost. As collaborators, we need to keep in mind what exactly we are trying to achieve.

As Lynne Snead and Joyce Wycoff tell us,

> Relationships are the foundation of collaboration. To
> have a healthy foundation, an environment should be
> one of mutual trust and respect, shared values and
> commitment, and appropriate recognition and rewards.

When we begin to develop a story, we often begin with just an image, or a setting, or a character. From that starting point, we talk and talk and talk for extended periods of time, exploring the image's potential meaning, or the setting's function in the telling of the story, or the character's strengths and weaknesses, aspirations and fears.

We never agree on every point, but we listen and weigh out the possibilities.

Understand the value of valuing differences.

As we talk, we keep in mind that the creative powers of our partner are different from our own. Valuing those differences gives each of us the opportunity to realize that *my own* vision is not necessarily the best way to proceed. It forces each of us to remember that *my own* way is certainly not the only way.

This doesn't mean that we are going to be a doormat in this relationship. As Edward Marshall tells us, in "using a collaborative process, we recognize the fundamental role played by basic values like respect, trust, self-esteem, and integrity." In collaborating, we must communicate our ideas and visions clearly, but without single-minded arrogance. In doing so, we have to push ourselves to recognize potential differences in the receiver of our message.

Face it, we're not all alike. There is an entire spectrum of personality traits that we embody and that we face in a potential partner. Where do we fall on the scale of being extroverted or introverted? Are we planners, or are we spontaneous? Are we logical or intuitive? Are we detail oriented, or are we *big picture* people? Is our focus on principles or on harmony? Are we regimented in our thinking, or are we flexible? Do we accept our life as it is, or are we ambitious to change it?

Understanding the mix of personality traits that make us who we are and accepting our partner for the person he or she is will provide a key to smooth collaboration.

We've all heard the saying, "Opposites attract." In our own case, we've found that this is not completely true. There are so many ways in which we are alike. Still, in taking a close look at our strengths and weaknesses, we have tried to see where we are different, accept the differences, and then capitalize on each other's strengths.

For example, one thing we've found is that we're both extroverts, to some extent. Because we are aware of that, however, and have tried to be conscious of the needs we each have in that regard, it has not hampered our ability to work together. To show you what we mean, we have listed below the polar ends of the spectrum regarding the characteristics of extroverted and introverted individuals. Take a moment and see where are you and your (potential) partner are situated on this scale.

Extroverts

- Focus on people and things.
- They try to change the world.
- Relaxed and confident.
- Understandable, usually accessible.
- Act before thinking.
- Seek variety and action.
- Prefer company.
- Prefer interests that have breadth.

Introverts

- Focus on concepts and ideas.
- They try to understand the world.
- Reserved and questioning.
- Subtle, often impenetrable.
- Think before acting.
- Seek quiet for concentration.
- Prefer solitude.
- Prefer interests that have depth.

Most of us fall somewhere in between these opposing characteristics.

Nikoo, for example, needs "quiet for concentration" *and* "variety and action." She wears earplugs to buffer the noise of the normal family free-for-all, which she also keeps track of as she writes and plots and answers email and thinks of book promotions.

Jim, on the other hand, prefers absolute solitude for

writing. And we use this to our advantage, planning our day and even our workspace to allow for these preferences. But when we consider the mix of all of the characteristics, we know that we both fall on the extroverted side.

Understand your differences and use them to the team's advantage.

Dixie Browning and Mary Williams, who have written over a dozen historical novels together under the pen name Bronwyn Williams, wrote to us about their similarities and differences.

> We're sisters. We both live on North Carolina's Outer Banks. We both have children, grandchildren, and retired husbands. As a Coast Guard wife, Mary traveled and lived in a number of exotic places. Dixie, whose background is art, has lived in the same house for forty-nine years.

Dixie hates doing research when a story's flowing and claims to have a short attention span, while Mary loves research and likes to do a "roadmap" of the plot.

Dixie is an early riser. She does her best work between 8:00 AM and noon. Mary is a late starter. She does her most productive work in the evenings.

Dixie is regimented, and Mary is not.

If we tried to pigeonhole them based on their work habits and preferences, we couldn't possibly fit either of them into a stereotypical mold. Human beings are too complex for that, and if we want to work with a partner, we would do well to continually remind ourselves of that fact.

Melissa Scott and Lisa Barnett are another team that

recognized early on how their differences are a resource.
Lisa told us,

> Melissa and I complement each other perfectly, and we
> pull each other up. She is simply phenomenal in making
> a place, a society, come crystal clear in a very few words.
> I'm very good with voice and character. She was a
> history major – her research is stunning. I was an
> English major, with a strong theatre background ...
> which means, I guess, that I leave things to the last
> minute and improvise brilliantly. And she is more
> disciplined than I am, so that pulls me up to her level.
> For me it's characters; for her, it's societies.

In these two teams of writers, the strengths of each
partner are maximized, and great stories are the result.
"Never," say Dixie and Mary, "lose sight of the goal,
writing the best book you can write. Recognize differences
in style, taste, and experience. That way you can *double* the
depth and breadth of your story."

Develop active listening skills.

On an intellectual level, we understand and respect the
differences in interests between people. But when it comes
right down to it, our human nature is always punching
holes in our good intentions, even when it comes to
listening.

In part, it goes back to our brain working six times
faster than our partner can speak. So here we are –
working in person or remotely – brainstorming plots or
discussing character motivation. Our partner is going on
enthusiastically about his or her idea. We got the first part
of it, but now, instead of listening carefully, we find

ourselves mentally dictating a letter to the editor in response to some outrageous article in the Sunday paper. Or we find ourselves blithely emptying the dishwasher.

It's even worse if our writing partner is a significant other or a family member. For some reason, the receiver wires seem to go dead very easily when we are listening to someone we live with *and* collaborate with.

But of course, there is a reason. If our collaborator is a life partner as well as a writing partner, we too often simply take them for granted. Hey, we know them inside and out. We *know* what they will think in most given situations and on most topics, and we dismiss their suggestions before they even offer them. That's wrongheaded on every level. The creative process is so unpredictable, and making assumptions about what your partner may come up with will surely prove self-defeating over the distance *and* over the short ground.

Many of us consciously work at getting along with our coworkers in a nine-to-five job. We strive continuously to create a productive atmosphere in which we can work. We even modify our behavior to attain some semblance of harmony in the work place. We should work *just* as hard at home. Just because we spend every moment of our time with this same partner, we have no justification for being careless or for tearing down their feelings.

It's probably true that the American flight to the suburbs was also a flight from the place where we work. Conditions in factories in the early part of last century were often horrible, and we probably felt that separating ourselves from them would give us a better quality of life. So we sought out more 'idyllic' settings of green lawns and better air.

Prior to that, however, people often worked in the place where they lived, whether it was on the farms or in the villages. Cottage industry is not a myth. Interestingly enough, whether it's due to pandemic or choice, more and more people are returning to a way of life where working from home is far more common than it was a few years ago. What we need to do now is to bring home the attitudes that foster harmony in the office or the shop. Tolerance and respect are especially essential in working with partner that you live with.

Be it blood kin, spouse, or significant other, when they're talking to you, don't let your eyes glaze over. You might just miss the best idea since *Crime and Punishment*.

Regarding feedback, say it, don't hide it.

Here, we've been preaching tolerance above and now we tell you, "Express your feelings. DON'T HOLD BACK."

Well, we do mean it, but we want you to *be gentle* as you respond to your partner's ideas and written work.

So how do you do it?

We suggest a two-step process that each partner must ascribe to:

1. Neither partner is allowed to get attached to unrevised work.
2. Work on developing a language – a code, really – that allows you to identify ideas and draft material that you absolutely cannot stand.

This is the way we do it. Each of us is working at opposite ends of the house on a different scene. After six grueling hours (well, maybe after an hour), we swap documents. This is where the detachment to unrevised work comes in. If we keep the mindset that this material is just a draft that we have churned out, that this is only the raw material from which a purer substance will be refined, then we have no reason to be defensive about any response to it. Of course, because this is always difficult, we need to be constantly reminding ourselves of the fact.

So, after swapping files, we read each other's work. If one of us is not happy with what the other did, she'll say sweetly, "Honey, that chapter that you wrote is very good, but I think we'll need to *fill it out* a little." Translation? "You'll have to give me a couple of hours to see if I can salvage *anything* from that pile of shit you just produced."

'Fill it out' is our code phrase for serious revising. Of course, you might say we're just kidding ourselves along, since we both know what 'fill it out' means. In fact, that is exactly what we're doing, and 'kidding' is the operative term. Kidding requires an element of good-naturedness and humor on both the transmitting and the receiving ends. This is what differentiates kidding from tormenting. A sense of humor is an important quality to retain and to nurture in a working relationship.

Interestingly enough, often the passage of time brings moments in a relationship when we both think and say the same thing simultaneously. This happens to us all the time – when we're writing, when we're giving workshops, and other times, as well. A reporter from the *New York Times* once commented that, during our interview with her, we cut in and out of each other's sentences without missing a beat. Still though, even at this comfort level, there are wrongful assumptions that we all can make – mistakes and miscommunications that inadvertently lead to hurt feelings. We need to be open to and conscious of our partner's individual creative powers.

One more thing. What do you do when your partner does not show the appropriate enthusiasm for an idea that you suggest? This is more likely to happen early in a project, when the two of you are less apt to be in the same groove on a project than you will be toward the end of a story.

Maybe the incident goes like this. You have a great premise and setting for a novel, you have a pretty good idea about who the main characters are, and you even have a resolution for the major conflict. You haven't thought the whole thing through, but you want to run the idea by your partner. So he listens, asks a few questions, and then says with a marked lack of enthusiasm, "Sounds like it has potential, but I don't think it's a story that I could add much to."

Disappointed, you calmly and rationally consider nailing his tongue to the kitchen table, but then decide that every story idea isn't going to be exciting for both of you. Something in the back of your brain, however, is telling you that you may simply have done a poor job 'pitching' it to your partner.

Don't let that idea slip away. Take a half hour. Write out as much of the idea as you can, as thoroughly as you can, and put it away. Three things could happen.

First, you might take a look at it in a week, in a month, or in a year and realize that it *wasn't* a very good idea. Not likely, but a possibility.

Second, you might someday write the story on your own or with another partner.

Third, if the idea has something to it, and it's given time to percolate in your partner's subconscious, the concept might just come back to the table. It might be modified or have some additions, but so what? Good ideas are good ideas. They often nag at us until we give them the attention they deserve.

In this case, you planted a seed that rattled around and finally took root amid the rocks in your partner's head.

So what does this all come down to?

Listening with an open mind. Making your responses constructive, rather than negatively critical of the glaring flaws. And when the responses to your ideas and prose are not entirely enthusiastic, forcing yourself not to be overly defensive of your efforts.

The building foundation of collaboration has to be set on solid grounds of communication, trust, respect. It is truly amazing what can come of it. Lynn Kerstan told us of a collaboration she did with fellow novelist Alicia Rasley:

> From a vague concept to an intricate story, brainstorming with Alicia was one of the most enjoyable and rewarding experiences I've had as a writer.

The book she was referring to went on to win several national awards.

This could be you.

4

A Match Made in Heaven
OR, BURNING DOWN THE HOUSE

PERHAPS IT WAS one of those ancient gods. Mercury. Or Bragi, the son of Odin. Or Elegba, the trickster god of the Yoruba. It may also have been some lesser ethereal creature, like that nearly transparent sprite with the spattered wings, perched grumpily on the antique ink pot and eyeing your keyboard right now. Or maybe it was simply pure coincidence, if you believe in such things.

Whatever caused you two star-crossed writers to come together, the fact is, here you are. Two of you, sold on the idea that, as Edward Marshall says, "collaboration is the way people naturally want to work." It's the way you want to work.

Well, you can count on one thing. These first days will test your relationship. These early forays into collaborative creation are really a series of giant steps that can crush a budding friendship or launch you *through* the "dating" process and leave you striding comfortably along the path to a permanent and productive relationship. Lynn Kerstan sent along this advice:

Don't enter lightly into a collaboration. Especially when writing fiction, it is an intense relationship. But when it works, it can be wonderfully rewarding. Writing is usually a solitary endeavor, and being able to share the ups and downs is terrific.

So we're ready. We confess to our writers' group that the romantic image of the solitary artist starving in a freezing attic no longer appeals to us. The vision of hot-blooded discussions between two vibrantly creative thinkers, wrestling with superior plot devices and characters who practically leap off the page – *that* is what fires our imaginations now.

Body and soul, we are together, armed and ready to do battle with any obstacle lying in our path.

Do it now. Lose the focus on *I*. Refocus on *WE*.

This is the stage when you need to shed the *me* mentality and learn the meaning of *us*. This is not *my* work, *my* idea, *my* individual effort; this is *our* work, *our* idea, *our* combined effort. We truly believe that when it comes to collaboration this is the most fundamental requirement in the transformation of the individual writer's perspective. We've all heard that cliched old saying, "There's no *I* in TEAM." Well, it's worth repeating.

Resign your charter membership in Egotists Anonymous.

Ego. That three-letter word that can cause such greatness and also such mischief. We're not psychologists, and we're not speaking in strictly psychoanalytic terms. But it doesn't require an advanced degree to know that some of us successfully achieve adulthood with relatively high self-esteem, while others of us do not. Some of us waltz through life with great, healthy egos, while some of us were apparently in the wrong line when that part of the psyche was being handed out.

No matter. We know we have some talent. We know we have the ability to work hard, even if it is only for short spurts. Whatever nature or temperament or constitution we've been blessed with, we are who we are. And when we look in the mirror, there is a *relatively* talented and *relatively* hardworking individual with dreams and aspirations staring back at us. Bestselling authors and Nobel Laureates have exactly the same experience when they look in the mirror.

It's important to remember that when it comes to collaboration, we are not expected to do a personality changeover. Instead, we simply need to focus on melding our talents and our efforts, *as they are,* with those of our partner. But if our ego sometimes gets out of control, we just need to focus on how to rein in the disruptively self-focused elements of our psyche.

And how do we do that?

Lee Rouland, a mystery and fantasy writer, offered this advice:

> Don't fall in love with your words. Abandon ego. Have fun. Chocolate helps.

Words of wisdom that are both practical and appetizing.

Interestingly enough, the collaborative teams we interviewed for this book kept bringing up the subject of the ego again and again.

Regarding the e-word, Cynthia Serra, who wrote paranormal novels with longtime friend Beth Ciotta, told us,

> There are two things that will affect this relationship
> more than anything else: chemistry and ego. I'm
> assuming that if you're considering a particular partner,
> you already have the chemistry. It's not something you
> can fabricate. It's either there or it's not. If you're not
> sure, then you might want to reconsider your choice (and
> your impetus for seeking a partner).
>
> Also, we've all seen those old "Leggo my Eggo"
> commercials. Well, *Leggo your Ego*. If not, you'll only
> create a hostile environment, and your partner will begin
> to think you don't trust her. Don't risk losing your friend.
> As our friend Sandy likes to say, "Check your ego at the
> door." Don't burn yourself.

Cynthia and Beth both assert that neither of them has an overly large ego, so when it comes to collaborating, their communication channels were relatively unobstructed by e-word complications.

But many of us *have* strong egos. We're not necessarily talking about inflated ones. We're talking about confidence, and self-esteem, and an element of pride in who we are and what we produce. However, we're also talking about the power source that feeds that sensitivity and defensiveness about our work. It is what is behind the lashing out that we sometimes do when our work gets criticized.

And what is the wisdom we've managed to gather from other collaborative writers?

> The important thing is not to let egos become involved.
> Try to remember that you're a team, and that you're
> working together to achieve a joint goal.

– Cindy Oberle

> Because we respect each other and put our egos on hold,
> we managed to avoid creative differences. Writers
> generally want to control their own work. It's a major
> adjustment to let someone else have an equal say. If ego
> gets in the way, the collaboration will fall apart.
> – Lynn Kerstan

> Our own egos were sacrificed unconditionally to the goal
> of good writing.
> – Lea Tassie

There it is.

The meddling of our egos in the creative process – and
the defensiveness that results – can have a negative impact
and even end the collaboration at an early stage in the
game. Overbearing pride in what you contribute must be
subdued and replaced with a more open, cooperative
spirit. If this can be accomplished, if that spirit of open-
ness can be infused into the communication process, then
the focus of our energy can be *on the product*, rather than *on
ourselves*. The process of listening and feedback can then be
so much more constructive.

Phil Taggart, who puts together the Arcade Poetry
Series with other writers groups, says:

> Good collaborators listen to each other. They're clear
> about what they want to get out of it. They keep their
> egos out of the process – it's not going to be any one's
> main show.

Before we move from this discussion, we'd like to share

with you what Louie Dillon and JB Hamilton Queen wrote
to us regarding the issue.

> We have big egos but have learned that we must
> abandon them in the writing place. Ego, however, is a
> powerful tool. It will force you to do your best.
> We both praise and criticize each other's work.
> When criticizing, we are careful to do so in a positive
> manner; pointing out the good, then suggesting how it
> could be made better.

We also believe that ego is indeed a powerful tool. We
believe in the value of sustaining the individual's self-
esteem, in the importance of a realistic perception of self-
worth. We all need it.

In choosing to pursue a career in writing and publishing, we are subjecting ourselves to potential onslaughts to
our confidence and to the disparagement of our talent:

Is the work good enough?
Will an editor like it?
Will an agent be able to sell it?
Why is this revision letter so damned long?
What will the critics' response be?
Will readers buy it?
Can I write a story as good as the last one?

All along the line, we are constantly faced with the
possibility of a negative response or rejection. Having a
healthy ego, knowing that we're made of tough stock,
knowing that we will not be completely crushed by the
disappointment du jour, is important for any writer.

But once again, we don't have to completely change

who we are. We just need to focus instead on moving from the *me* stage to *us* to make the collaboration process work.

Resign your charter membership to Annoyances, Inc.

The constant tapping of the pen on the table. Emptying the dishwasher. The nonstop crunch of cookies. The unsuccessful stifling of a yawn. Checking the phone every sixth heartbeat. The clicking of teeth. Resetting the height of the chair. The negative shaking of the head during a brainstorming session.

These are just a small sample of the plethora of annoyances that we can bring unconsciously to the collaborative workspace. Actually, these seemingly small nuisances appear to be the most critical when we are living with our collaborator or even spending large blocks of time with them, working on a specific task.

Well, put aside thinking of them as trivial nuisances. Even though these are things that we are often not even aware of doing, when it comes to working with someone else, these insignificant habits can often take center stage. And these little annoyances can lead to a battle scene on that stage to rival the one that "did afright the air at Agincourt."

> Jim tells me that I immediately begin shaking my head and frowning when he starts conveying an idea that I think might be unappealing to a general audience. I wasn't even aware that I do this, never mind the fact that I don't give him a fair chance to finish a thought that could win me over once we begin brainstorming the possibilities.

Nikoo tells me I yawn when she starts with her ideas, quickly blaming it on being overtired when she notices. But then she complains when I start eating – stuffing myself with chocolate chip cookies, she says – as soon as she really starts getting into a plot description.

I have to admit yawning and eating *could* be considered distractions. And if Nikoo were a wallflower – holding back from *gently* voicing her complaints about my behavior – I wonder how many story opportunities we might have lost along the way.

"Quit yawning."

"I'm buying you a neck brace if you don't get rid of that head shake."

"There are going to be some very sorry elves if you don't stop munching on those cookies."

If our partnerships are to have a reasonable chance of surviving, we need to discuss potential idiosyncrasies *before* they become a source of real trouble. Ask your partner if anything you do annoys her … while you both still have the sense of humor to deal with it.

To be productive we all need to be conscious of our little foibles and modify our behavior. Get those little quirks out into the open and then get rid of them (rather than defending them), so that you can move ahead without the distractions. There are so many more important things that you want to be focusing your efforts on.

Like writing, for instance.

Beyond the Rubble

We all know that history is a constant cycle of birth, flowering, death, and regeneration. The rise and the fall and the renaissance.

Ah, that sweet rebirth.

How often do we look back on periods of revitalization – such as Florence in the time of Michelangelo and Raphael – and marvel at the artistic accomplishments, the architecture. What is great from the past is preserved, hopefully, and complemented by what is new. That which lacks greatness is eradicated and replaced.

It happens over and over. It's almost as if we're hard-wired with the need to do it better. To make it stronger. To get it right.

This is why we revised this book. To revisit where we've been, assess how far we've come, relate what has changed.

The same principle works in this new venture we are embarking on called *collaboration*.

We are human, however, with all the flaws and idiosyncrasies and aspirations inherent in the species. Even more to the point, as writers we are individuals with unique creative visions and high expectations. So no matter how hard we try, there *will* be conflicts:

> We debated *a lot* about how scenes would develop, but it was just a bickering form of brainstorming. Now we laugh about "the mugging scene" and "the clutie scene" because we had such battles about them, and yet the book turned out fine anyway.
> – Alicia Rasley

> There have been times when we were so frustrated that we declared never to write another word together. That scary thought always jolted us back to reality.

We realize how lucky we are to have each other to bounce around scenarios and ideas, to say what works or what doesn't work. We agree that for either of us to write on our own would be like stumbling around in a dark forest, lost and without direction. As a writing *team*, we never have to face a blank page or take rejections alone.

– Louie Dillon and JB Hamilton Queen

People would hear us "working out plot problems" and then move sharp instruments out of our reach.

– Carol Reynard and Shirl Henke

No matter how mild-mannered we might be by nature, we all do it sometimes. We argue, we bicker, we threaten our partner with bodily harm. The truth is, though, that despite the chaos that often comes with such conflict, we usually learn from these skirmishes and build a stronger foundation, one formed with a consideration of our differences.

We always knew compromise would have to play a huge role in our efforts if our partnership were to work. But until we defined exactly which trail we would like to blaze (i.e., exactly what we wanted to write most), we kind of hopped all over the place.

– Lori & Tony Karayianni (AKA Tori Carrington)

Prior to crossing the publication line, Lori and Tony wrote a hard-boiled mystery and a thriller (to satisfy Tony's needs), two mainstream women's fiction works (to satisfy Lori's), and several other stories (to satisfy the curiosity of both of them). In their own words, until "those bumps we hit early on evened out," publication wasn't going to happen. As a collaborative team, they had to learn "how to compromise within the lines of each book."

Curiously enough, we had the same experience and hit the same kinds of bumps as we zigzagged blindly down that literary path prior to finding out what writing together could offer.

> Jim would write this beautiful prose, but there was not a single person in his stories that I could care about.

> Dialogue. Dialogue. Dialogue. Relationship. Dialogue again. That's all Nikoo cared about.

We argued. We listened. We compromised. Then we each took our strengths and brought them to the collaboration table, combining them to create fiction that was stronger than anything we'd ever created on our own.

Interestingly enough, many disagreements – and open conflict – do not necessarily occur in the initial stages of your collaboration. As we feel our way into the process – and as that "first-date" thrill fades into cherished memory – honesty and perceptiveness are the qualities required of the new partners. Each of us must stay 'tuned-in' to the developing relationship, ready to react when the first symptoms of strain or disharmony appear.

> In the early stages of writing, we had no timelines, no deadlines. Without those sorts of boundaries and without the establishment of a definite goal – as in, getting such and such a novel done by such and such a time – we had few, if any, disagreements. Once we decided to partner *for real* on a book, and to attempt to

> sell it, and to attempt to strive for a certain level of
> writing, that's when the hardships began.
> – Amy Ingram

What Amy and her partner experienced is a very
common occurrence in the collaboration experience. A lot
of writers see the concept of collaboration as the next
logical step beyond the critique group. In many ways it is,
but in most critique group situations, boundaries exist –
parameters that limit *personal* investment in a finished
product.

As we've said above, collaboration goes beyond that,
eliminating the boundaries between contributors. If the
two writers have not identified *in detail* their expectations
and priorities at the outset of working together, conflicts
are sure to arise. This is particularly true as the 'stakes' are
raised. Read that as the moment when the opportunity for
publication appears to be at hand.

So what are we to do?

In the following chapter, we identify deadline-related
conflicts as one item to be listed in a *Statement of Intent* letter
that you and your collaborator should draft together, agree
upon, and sign.

Beyond contractual agreements, however, collaborative
team members have to nurture a similar mindset comprised of
similar goals. For example, are we going to take an indefinite
amount of time (years? decades?) to write a 'classic' work of
fiction? Are we agreeing to finish this book-in-progress within
a specific period of time? Are we searching for fame based on
a single masterpiece? Are we striving to be good *and* prolific?

These are questions that no one can answer but you.
The plural *you*. In short, identifying what each of you will
contribute clarifies what *role* each of you will play in the

collaboration process. In the same way, being open enough to clearly define the team's goals up front, *before* the first blush of courtship fades, will allow you to create a united vision about where this artistic path will lead.

Often the development of a new relationship can be like a steeplechase on a wet afternoon. Danger, it seems, awaits at every turn. Truly, any number of obstacles can knock a horse down or sweep a rider from the saddle in the wink of an eye. Slippery slopes, hedgerows, low hanging branches.

While we were assembling the information for this chapter, Jim got a message in a fortune cookie that seemed oddly relevant. "Many receive advice; the wise hear it." Every one of the writing teams we interviewed for this book found some hedgerow or other that they needed to work themselves through. Regarding our own working relationship, we are true believers in the adage that "knowledge is power."

For us, the more of these obstacles we can foresee and work through without resorting to actual, full-blown conflict, the better we feel and the more energy we can save up for the important things, like the writing.

Allotting a specific amount of time and energy to each aspect of a job is something that is preached to us in the workplace. Prioritizing, allotting, delegating. When it comes to the creative process, however, we sometimes tend to think that this management of time has no relevance.

The initial disagreement had to do with our hero and
our own vision of the characters. For a while, we battled
with words, each 'favoring' our own characters through
our writing. One of the first things we had to do was to
agree on how much time and energy we were going to
give each character.

– Amy Ingram

In our own case, despite years of technical and
management training, we're worse than most people in this
regard. Interestingly enough, our biggest hang-up has
nothing to do with any attachment to a certain character.
Spending too much time researching minute details is our
downfall. We admit it. We enjoy researching.

But how much research is enough? It's a time-manage-
ment question we are often asked in workshops.

This is the way we think of it. The research needs to be
sufficient to support the characters' development in the
story. In a way it's like US currency. You only see the
phantom portrait of Andrew Jackson when you hold that
twenty dollar bill up to the light in a certain way. If you're
looking for it, it's there. But even if you're not, that special
element still says that the currency is genuine.

In our partnership, we each tell ourselves, you are the
writer. You have a good grasp of who your potential
readers are and what their range of expectations encom-
passes. In short, each of us needs to decide for ourself, but
we can't let research get in the way of actually writing the
story, either. Put another way, if we were going for that
dream job interview, we wouldn't spend so much time
primping in front of the mirror that we forget to arrive on
time.

So what is the short answer to "How much research is
enough?" Our answer is that you've researched enough

when your partner threatens to lock the bookcases, install controls on the Internet usage, and have you banned from the local library.

Discuss and set schedules. Allot your time. Expend energy with the end result in mind.

Sometimes we both write the same scene, and then have to choose [the better one]. But we've learned to save the discarded scene for later in the book ... or sometimes for a whole new book.
  – Bernice P. Picard

While the proposed solution might fall under a heading like "Waste Nothing," the issue is clearly one of communication. A scenario like this – where two collaborating partners write the same scene – is, of course, more likely to occur when the two writers might get together once or twice a week to discuss and swap their work. But we've done it, even though we live in the same house and discuss our work two or three or four times a day.

A number of times, we've come up with scenes that overlap or duplicate the action in a different way. In spite of this lapse in our lines of communication, we've always tried to accept the blunder with a good sense of humor. And as Lisa Barnett reminded us, writing the same scene is sometimes a necessary activity:

Even when you have a good, detailed plot as to who's doing what, sometimes you need to see how it reads from a different point of view (if you're using multiple points of view) or simply from a different angle in the room. Sometimes both authors will want to work on a particular scene, and you can then decide which version suits the story better.

Thorough and detailed communication plays an even more integral part in a long distance collaboration than in a partnership where the writers live in the same household. To maximize efficiency, there can be no surprises and a clear understanding of the team's jointly held goals.

Talk might be cheap, but time is money.

In those days, we printed out pages when we wanted to share them. We did spend a lot of money sending stuff through the mail.
— Cynthia Oberle

Indeed, to succeed in such a relationship, each of us has to come to an understanding of the value of our time and of the time we spend communicating *professionally*. And we're not using that word lightly. As a member of a collaborative team, you are engaging in the development of a professional relationship.

Part art, part business — collaborative writing comes with all the responsibilities and rewards found in any professional relationship.

It was damned irritating that friends would not acknowledge that we were working.
— Lee Rouland

Most of us realize that as writers we live in a different world than the rest of God's creatures. And because this other universe appears so lofty and ethereal to our friends and relatives and telemarketers, those earth dwellers believe it is their holy quest to drag us (out of our shoeboxes, actually) back into the muddle of daily existence.

There is nothing wrong with this, for any of the parties concerned. In fact, it's often a good thing. Face it, we all need to have a balance of realism and fantasy in order to create the best stories that we can. When these intrusions, however, cut into the precious time that we have put aside for our writing, watch out!

Nikoo faced with an entire battalion of these campaigners when she quit her day job and stayed home to write full time. Now, it didn't matter that, prior to quitting, she had been working sixty to seventy hours a week and had made a point of *telling* everyone that she was giving up her engineering job and staying home *to write*. It made no impression on anyone when she said she was not giving up her earlier work habits, that she was just changing careers, and her office was now going to be located at home.

Nikoo can stifle the urge to be industrious on the peripheral things around the house. It was the intrusions that were the problem. Being *home* meant to those around us that she was *available*. The writing that she intended to do…well, it would *naturally* take a back seat to everyone else's needs. At least, that's the way everyone around us saw it.

The other pressure comes from within. The two of us can very easily sit over coffee for an hour or two talking about anything but the project at hand. After all, we enjoy each other's company. So having and maintaining a disciplined attitude about our time is essential.

The bottom line is you have to tell it straight, as we did with our kids:

Unless there is smoke or blood or bone visible, interruptions are not acceptable.

There comes a time in every writer's life when, like it or not, we have to draw the line and become (at times) unapproachable. 'The Snob' is one colorful name that we can be labeled with. But we have to do it; we have to simply smile and retreat to the cave. Sometimes, we joke about the family as a mini wolf pack. Jim is the alpha-dog, and Nikoo is the alpha-bitch.

She started monitoring the calls through the answering machine (remember those things?). She didn't answer the door when the kids were at school. She scheduled all the volunteering and extra school activities into one day a week...as much as possible. In spite of doing all of this, she still was not able to get together sixty to seventy hours a week. Then she had a tremendous revelation. She really didn't need that many work hours...*if* she could have large blocks of writing time. And that was exactly what she was able to get.

Now, twenty-five years later, Nikoo has regained the friendship of the same people who once felt slighted. And she has their respect. Respect for who she is, respect for her career, and respect for her schedule.

Jim, on the other hand, has simply become a bit more thick-skinned about outsiders' comments, sometimes even playing up his "easy" life in responding to those who feel compelled to tease him.

So pull up the drawbridge. Fill the moat. Don't be afraid to be the bad guy. Set the rules, stick to them yourself, and other people eventually learn to accept them.

The only irritations came from factors outside of the writing process/partnership, when Real Life demands

like family and other obligations put our schedules out
of sync.
    – Lynn Kerstan

Writing together requires some sense of timing.
Depending on how we work as a team, that timing will
differ. The timing required for side-by-side work is quite
different from a process in which one partner will draft,
while the other follows and revises. However we do it, the
collaborative team members must function like gears in a
machine. The teeth in those gears must mesh.

As communicative and resolute as we can be, 'real life'
sometimes cannot be avoided, and those gears can clash,
grind, jerk that writing machine to a halt. Things happen
that we just cannot plan for. Illnesses, tragedies, and even
wildly wonderful things occur.

There was a time when the two of us were approached
to collaborate on a musical version of *The Scarlet Pimpernel*.
Discussions went forward, but then a contract for a trilogy
of novels pulled us in another direction. Because of life's
circumstances, we couldn't get the timing down on that
particular three-way collaborative effort.

Even when we are committed to a project, the hand of
fate has its own way of wreaking havoc on our day-to-day
schedules and even long-term plans. When it does, all we
can do is to be understanding of our partner and try to do
what we can to help him or her through the difficulties.
This is where common sense and a compassionate human
nature takes precedence over any advice a writing book on
collaboration can give you.

In the early stages, we were riffing on a creative
adrenaline high, so I found very few irritations. And
throughout the process, we've remained good friends –

which is pretty much consistent with other collaborations
I've done.
   – David Nickle

David's experience is one that we all should consider
striving toward. When we're high on creative adrenaline,
and the work is flowing, nothing seems to matter. There
are no annoyances. 'Irritation' is only a four-syllable word
found in the dictionary.

And how do we get that creative adrenaline flowing in
our veins and in our partner's veins without drawing the
attention of the local narcotics squad?

Provide positive feedback.

Good news does it, to be sure. Of course, the downside
of it is that good news is something we cannot control. Still
though, when the moment comes and we are able to
convey that positive comment, the creative level is certain
to rise. Jim's mother says, "Success breeds success."

We had only the synopsis and first three chapters of
our first collaborative novel done when we sent it out to the
prospective agents. Five days later, when we received a call
from a literary agent in California, excited about our work
and inquiring to see the rest of it, we pushed our creative
gears into overdrive. A very respected agent was excited
about us, and about our story and our characters. Of *course*
we could finish the novel in no time. The creative juices
were pumping.

Just as in David Nickle's experience, we immediately
became too wrapped up in the project to take notice of
anything counterproductive, anything that might slow
down our writing. The defining value of nearly every
working communication became ... if it wasn't relevant to

producing more story for the growing number of pages, then it didn't deserve a discussion. We finished that work in the same amount of time that it took us to write the first three chapters.

To this day, we still use positive feedback as a motivational tool, whether it be a good review of one of our books or email from a fan in New Zealand or a letter from a thoughtful reader in Texas just saying, "Howdy!" and inquiring about our next work. Knowing that someone is excited about what we're trying to do is always certain to keep us forging ahead in the right direction. And in between times, we make a point of telling one another what we like about the work that's being done.

Set goals and meet them.

Planning and goal-setting are a vital element of a thriving creative partnership. Though every one of us may not be a natural planner, lasting success does not happen by chance.

When the two of us started our collaboration, we each brought to the partnership ideas, some talent, and a good-humored approach to dealing with natural disasters and cosmic adversity. Maybe it was the engineer in her, but Nikoo brought something else, as well – a notebook and a calendar.

The notebook was for jotting down everything important and anything trivial that might have some relevance to the project. The calendar was for setting schedules and imposing deadlines, even when there *were* no deadlines.

Years later and after many changes to our evolving method of collaboration, we still are devoted to the notebook and calendar. We use them for keeping track of information and creating deadlines that beat our publisher's needs. We use a spread sheet to monitor our daily goals and output.

The numbers that mark our progress are tremendously useful in motivating ourselves. Writing a thousand words a day. Writing two thousand a day. Looking up our deadline on the calendar and cutting a month from it and dividing the number of days into the number of words.

"Jim, we have to write 1527 words a day, working seven days a week."

No, we are not sick. And no, we are not obsessed. We have discovered a motivational tool that helps us to keep our creative wheels turning.

Creating a story is a process. George Bernard Shaw put it this way,

Imagination is the beginning of creation. You *imagine* what you desire; you *will* what you imagine; and at last you *create* what you will.

Processes need to be managed. As a team, we must agree upon a strategic plan that will allow us to meet the goals we have set for ourselves. Lack of goal-setting actually impedes the process, forcing both members of the team to work in a fog, without direction and without the opportunity to receive positive reinforcement for ongoing work.

As you will see in the next chapter, we are firm believers in setting both long-term and short-term goals. For our purposes here, though, suffice it to say that tools such as a notebook and the calendar help us monitor our progress in achieving our goals. In using these valuable tools, we eliminate the sudden panic of the looming deadline, as well as many irritations and disagreements that so often create setbacks in a collaborative team's efforts.

Stimulate friendly competition

Consider harnessing the competitiveness latent in every creative partnership. What can be better than a bit of *healthy* competition to stimulate creativity and productivity. By this we mean setting goals together and then comparing – in a friendly manner – to see if we each met them. We're big on this during the days when we are both plugged into our computers.

I'll write 1500 unrevised words by three o'clock.

Good for you. I'll do ten pages of revision by noon.

A number of collaborating partners we know challenge each other in all-out writing sprints. Some even go away together on writers' retreats for a weekend or for a week, and all they do is write, write, write.

What? Should we sacrifice the *quality* of our work to this rivalry for mere *quantity*? Of course not. In our case, we call it the productivity game. And we *know* it's a game. We also know that the revision stage will follow.

And in the end, there are many days we don't meet our goal because of the extra time we might need to work the draft of a passage – or to do an unexpected bit of research. But then, as with most writers, the more we do, the easier the writing becomes.

When any of us start to write, building that creative flow and stamina is a gradual process. We wouldn't go out and run ten miles on the first day of getting back into shape. We do, however, need to start somewhere, and setting an achievable goal is the answer. Staring at a blank screen for fifteen minutes today can easily lead to fifteen minutes of writing tomorrow and an hour the next day and four hours – and maybe, eight hours a day – by the end of a month. Through good-natured competition between partners who have the same goals in mind, we are each encouraging the other to sit in front of that computer and keep tapping at that keyboard.

Hey, whatever works to get the creative adrenaline flowing and to keep it flowing.

We have suggested many things in this chapter that need to be considered. So what are the most critical aspects of starting and developing a collaborative relationship?

- Continuous communication
- Positively directing the forces of one's ego
- Controlling idiosyncratic behavior
- Being consciously sensitive to our partner's needs
- Managing conflict
- Managing time
- Setting achievable goals

Whatever your situation, this early stage of collaboration is the most critical time. Work through it, survive it, learn from it, and you find yourself on a path that gets easier and easier with the passage of time.

If we think back on the early stages of any relationship – like dating – many of us will recall that the most difficult moments center on that difficulty in communicating. The anxiety and the awkwardness in trying to find the right words to say, in expressing our feelings, in trying to reach a comfort level where each person can get to know the other a little better.

We hear all the time from partners who have worked together for years and have produced a good number of quality books. Nearly every one of them says that good communication is a part of their way of life – as important as their combined talent and their individual craft skills, as essential as a shared goal.

The Prenuptial Agreement

> Live together like brothers,
> and do business like strangers.
> *– Arabic Proverb*

WHILE WE ARE NOT absolute proponents of such a sentiment, the concept has some relevance when we consider the formation of this odd mixture of the personal relationship and the professional or business alliance.

The idea of a prenuptial agreement between two people about to be married may sound a little unromantic to most of us. But it is not illogical, particularly when we are talking about the marriage of minds that must occur in the collaborative relationship. As the inimitable Mrs. Malaprop says in Sheridan's *The Rivals*:

'tis safest in matrimony to begin with a little *aversion*.

If not 'aversion,' certainly *'clarity'* is an important element in a successful relationship.

Whether we begin a collaborative relationship with the idea that we'll be writing together on one project, or whether we are planning to write together forever, we all must think clearly about the future. We're talking about the period *beyond* the artistic molding of ideas, *beyond* the careful crafting and revising of a story.

When the Association of Artist's Representatives (AAR) took up the question in a 1992 meeting, they recommended that writing partners have a clear business agreement prior to working together:

> A collaboration agreement must deal with termination of the collaboration: How the collaborators can part ways, who keeps the money, who keeps the rights to the material. This is comparable to deciding before you get married who will have custody of the kids.

It's not with the end in mind that most people enter into a relationship. As we open this chapter about collaboration agreements, however, we want to stress that the better we are able to record each partner's business expectations and responsibilities, the better prepared we will feel. After all, it is almost inescapable that business questions will arise sometime during a successful collaboration.

To start, raising the question of a need for an agreement should not be construed as mistrusting your partner. If we were to buy a house with our best friend, we would have a lawyer draw up a contract. Why should it be, then, that when it comes to the investment of time and creative energy – far more precious commodities than real estate – we get the jitters and feel disloyal for even bringing up the subject?

Put simply, the answer is that we shouldn't feel either jittery or disloyal. If we view our writing as more than a hobby, if we are striving to publish our work, then we should behave as the professionals we are.

Draft a fair agreement, sign it, and get it out of the way. It's for the good of everyone concerned.

While some collaborative teams we know have gone off to lawyers, Lynn Kerstan and Alicia Rasley decided early in their collaboration that a letter of agreement would suffice. David Nickle's agreements with his various collaborators on a number of projects were worked out through his publisher. Lea Tassie and Kathleen Webb drafted their own collaboration agreement to try to keep the responsibilities fairly balanced and clearly defined.

All of these teams worked out their professional arrangements in advance, in order to avoid a situation such as the one Agatha Christie referred to when she quipped,

> When you collaborate with someone, you get all of the headaches and half of the royalties.

In our own case, having been happily married for decades, we think of everything as jointly held. Still, when it comes to our dealings with publishers, the wording of the each contract provides that all payments will be split equally between us.

In case of independent publishing, some distributors will split payments, but not all.

Now, to clarify the purpose of the collaboration agreement, we need to remember that the agreement's purpose is not *solely* the distribution of money. Many other facets of the writing partnership exist that can become reasons for a dispute. We will try to list as many as we can.

Before we get started, though, please remember that

what we are providing below is not legal advice; only a lawyer can provide that. What we're attempting to give you is just some basic information that collaborators can use to start their discussion.

As far as the agreement itself, it could be as simple as a letter signed by both collaborators. It could also be what Hal Zina Bennett and Michael Larsen, in their book *How to Write with a Collaborator,* refer to as a "Statement of Intent." By their definition, this statement "defines your responsibilities prior to the sale of the book to the publisher."

There are many scenarios that we've listed below, but as we draft the agreement, we can put as much or as little information as we like into it. Depending on how detailed we get, we should consider the document a kind of checklist for discussing and smoothing out potential ruts in the collaborative road.

In March of 1992, Peter Skolnik, AAR counsel and a practicing attorney, offered his advice on the subject at an AAR general meeting. Essentially, his suggestion was to find a way to resolve – in advance and in writing – the work responsibilities, financial responsibilities, and the issues dealing with the future of the specific work and the partnership. He itemized his list roughly as follows:

- Contributions to the project

What is it that each member of the collaborative team will be bringing to the project?
Do both of you write?
Is one responsible for research?

Is one of you to be responsible for the "business" aspects or for the promotion of the work?

As ever evolving as the roles might be, we each will play a specific role – actually, several roles – in the collaboration process. We ourselves have found that our specific responsibilities have never really been completely defined, since each of us will do anything and everything to get the job done. But then, this may not hold true in every collaborative team.

There are partnerships in which one partner does only the research and editing. There are others, more so in the case of nonfiction teams, where one partner might only provide expertise. Sometimes, a ghostwriter will do the writing for a celebrity or an established author in a work-for-hire situation.

Clear definition of responsibilities should be included as a key part of any collaborative agreement.

- Schedules

Is there a set time put aside to finish the project?

Are there deadlines for revisions or are they open-ended?

How many rounds of revisions are expected? Is there a specified limit?

One member of a collaborative team wrote to us about how a lack of any agreement regarding the scheduled completion of a work-in-progress pushed their working relationship to an unpleasant edge:

It was clear we were on 'thin ice' in the last stages of completing the novel, although I knew we would complete it together. After an editor requested seeing our work, I pushed to get the completed novel to the editor within a month (we had about one-quarter of the novel left to write).

I worked like crazy on my chapters, with my edits, to do this. Circumstances did not allow my partner to complete her work within the same schedule. I became very frustrated and found myself writing 'her' chapters. She, in turn, became frustrated with me because she felt I was usurping her role in the novel. The tension was palpable every time we talked on the phone. I'd ask her with dread, "So, how much do you have done?" And she'd reply tersely, "Not as much as you'd like. I've been busy."

Without saying as much, we kept our final month working together purely business, each knowing inside that we couldn't continue to work this way. To me, we sent the novel to the editor *late*; to my partner, we sent it to her *at our earliest convenience*.

Their friendship somehow survived, but their future plans for collaboration needed a breather.

Schedule insensitivity is one of the most common complaints within collaborative writing teams, and good communication does not always provide a solution to this problem.

The power of the written word – or in this case, the date on a written document – may provide another possible approach. From the time we are very young, we are culturally conditioned to believe in the written word and to be controlled by the authority behind it.

Consider for a moment a solitary passerby who stops on a whim at a yard sale. Our impromptu shopper spots a rather attractive, albeit chipped and discolored coffee cup. Upon being asked, the yard sale proprietor mentions that she will part with the heirloom for a dollar. Now, in most cases, our shopper will *bargain* boldly over the price before purchasing the item. All very well and good.

If, however, that same intrepid shopper were to walk into an antique store and see exactly the same piece with a printed price tag attached to it, what will be the response? What about if the price tag had the added authority of a national pricing system behind it, as in the case of a major chain of stores? Well, who in their right mind would dare to question the price, never mind *haggle*?

The truth is that most of us shy away from questioning a printed price tag. We either quietly pay the full amount, or we don't buy the item. And why is that? Is it just that we know the store clerk hasn't the *authority* to change the written price? Or are we all so socially conditioned to acquiesce to the printed word that we are afraid to object, afraid to be seen as operating outside of the 'normal' constraints of consumerism, with its acceptance of pre-determined, printed prices?

The answer to all of this lies, very simply, in the power of written word. If it is written down, then we believe it must be unchangeable, perhaps even 'gospel.' And we're not using that term lightly. Even the religious texts of Judeo-Christian culture are steeped in terms like "the Covenant," and "the power of the Word," and "the Word made Flesh." Academics call it the *logo*centricity of our culture.

This is not, however, a book aimed at questioning our society's core values. Our intention is not even to make life more difficult for the poor sales clerk making somewhere around minimum wage in a store. Rather, what we are trying to do in this section is to make you aware of, and enable you to take advantage of, the power that lies within the written word.

Who says that the publishers are the only ones who can contractually mandate completion dates? Why shouldn't we, as collaborators, discuss and *document* the same kind of restriction on schedules? Actually, since *we* are now the ones documenting it in our agreement letter, there is a much better chance that the book will get done within the schedule we've decided upon and written down.

Remember, an oral agreement will not suffice. The power lies in the *written* word.

- **Finances**

While in most cases publishing contracts would ordinarily divide payments to the collaborative team equally, the collaborative agreement still should clearly state how the income should be divided from the various categories of rights and subsidiary rights. In some cases, depending on the amount of work assigned to each collaborative team member, a different type of arrangement could be decided upon before the work goes forward.

- **Copyright ownership**

Again, as long as the work does not fall into the category of 'work-for-hire,' the copyright should ideally reflect both of the collaborators' names, unless other arrangements are decided upon and recorded in the collaborative agreement.

Whatever the nature of the relationship, provision should be made for just who would own the copyright and how the rights are to be divided in the event of the collaboration terminating before publication.

> Will one party have the right to use the other's work
> product, and on what terms?

We have a friend who is in her eighties. When we first met her at a local writers' chapter meeting, she told us that she had once collaborated on a short story for a magazine contest with a woman whom she had been friends with for almost her entire adult life. The story didn't win the contest, and the manuscript was relegated to the desk drawer.

Years later, our friend happened to find her notes for the story in an old notebook. She rewrote the story from scratch, using virtually nothing from the original collaborative effort, and then was delighted to see it included in an area arts publication that is distributed for free at the local supermarkets and libraries and senior citizens center. She received no financial compensation for the story. Her friend, however, happened to see the story in the publication.

Even though the story was entirely different from the one they had worked on together, the friendship was over.

This item would be an insignificant point in a healthy and thriving collaborative partnership. Like everything else, however, a matter such as deciding who is free to develop unpublished material deserves at least *some* attention up front.

• Approvals and Controls

We hear collaborative teams say it frequently, the work

is not done until we are both satisfied with the project. We speak of the joint venture. The team spirit. But then, what if the authors' differences over a project are greater than their patience? Who has the last word?

Edo Van Belkom – prolific author of science fiction, fantasy, horror, and mystery stories – was also the winner of the Bram Stoker Award for a story he collaborated on with David Nickle. Edo wrote to us about the first stages of their work on "Rat Food," the story that went on to win the prestigious national award:

> We decided that I'd write the first half and Dave would write the second. I took a few days with it and wrote about eight pages or so, then passed them along to Dave. He took what I'd written home with him and wrote the second half of the story THAT NIGHT.
>
> The next morning he proudly thrust the manuscript at me as if it were a fistful of dollar bills. The smile on his face said, "Finished." But of course it wasn't finished. Both of us knew that the story had only been begun.

Although Dave and Edo had no problem moving on to the revision process and working on their project for as long as it took to complete it to their satisfaction, their situation held the makings of very real conflict.

The pride writers have in doing an incredible amount of work in such a short time, the gratification and the sense of accomplishment that we feel, often charges us up, making it very difficult to slow down and accept a partner's studied critique of our work. We don't always separate in our minds a critique of our *work* and a critique of our *efforts*.

Nonetheless, this matter of approvals does not only

include an agreement on which partner or partners have the final say on the work; there is also the issue of how and when this right is to be exercised.

Does the right exist only at the manuscript stage?
At the editorial revision stage?
At the galley proof stage?
What about in the case of a new edition or a reprinting?
And what about the subsidiary rights of audiobooks, translations, serializations, or film?

Again, this might seem to be a petty point of discussion for an active and thriving writing team. But again, it never hurts to put these matters on the table and avoid problems down the road.

- Sequels

New York literary agent Donald Maass addresses the issue of collaborative teams and sequels in his book, *The Career Novelist*:

Usually this is no problem: the collaborators write sequels together. But that's not always possible or practical. One partner may have prior contract commitments, or may simply be bored with the project. What happens then? Unless your agreement spells out a procedure, there could be delays, sore feelings, and lost income.

This problem is not as farfetched as we might think at first. In any kind of genre writing, for example, devoted readers get hooked on multi-volume adventures, family sagas, and specific historical characters who show up in a series of stories.

Our own experience taught us that early on. We were no sooner done with our first novel, *The Thistle and the Rose*, when the idea of utilizing one of the secondary characters for the next book struck us as a very attractive idea. Our readers agreed, and we have since completed many tales that connect, in some way, with that original work.

So again, talk it out. Issues such as these are hardly insurmountable if we just keep in mind our priorities and use a little common sense. As Donald Maass says,

> Be generous. If one of you wishes to continue but the other does not, why not let the series go forward?
>
> Some authors are afraid their children will grow up into monsters that they cannot control and do not recognize, but if you are that hung up on control why collaborate in the first place? Others are worried about money. They feel they should profit from what they helped to make. Well, why not?
>
> Work out something equitable. Cut your partner in even if she cuts out. That's a lot better than not being able to profit at all.

Not too many people build a career or get rich on one book. Careers and income are generally built on a series of works. How far would Debbie Dadey and Marcia Thornton Jones have gone if they had stopped writing after producing one *Bailey School Kids* story?

So don't overlook the value of future works or the usefulness of agreements on them. They may provide a gold mine of opportunities and income.

- Project expenses

Hey, we're talking money here, so pay attention. Actually, it's not just about money, but still stay tuned. To be honest, there are many areas that could be covered under this heading, but we'll try to list the major items that we think are worth considering.

1. Pre-publication expenses

Unless you have a generous employer who is willing to absorb the cost of marketing your collaborative endeavors, these expenses can create a serious drain in the healthiest of writing budgets. So discuss it up front. How are these expenses are to be divided? What are the ceilings?

We need to discuss the budget and consider the potential outlay of money that might prove pricey: research materials, books, videos, trips, assistants. Updated equipment? Or computer software? Or even an electric typewriter for the Latter Day Luddites lurking out there?

2. Post-publication expenses

For most published writers, this is the black hole of the publishing costs. If we want, we can continuously shell out money for such promotional expenses as 'swag', giveaways, mailing lists, advertising campaigns, booksignings, book tours, blog tours, contests. The list goes on and on, and faster than we could give you ideas on how to spend your advance, your nest egg, your inheritance, the kids' college fund, the church bingo money (just kidding), the expense dollars can add up.

Needless to say, this is one area where a promotional

budget – clear and *recorded* – is a must. Lynn Kerstan found this out from experience and sent this specific advice:

> I was eager to promote, and Alicia considered promotion on the level we could afford to be pretty much a waste of time. (She was probably right.) We ought to have discussed it beforehand.
>
> Ultimately, we came to an acceptable compromise. To avoid potential conflict, the level of commitment to promotion – financial and otherwise – should be written into the contract.

- Agents, lawyers, and publishers

Depending on the level of individual collaborator's past involvement with agents, lawyers, and publishers, this could be a minor point, or a very complicated one. In terms of agents and lawyers, it all comes down to who does what if each collaborator has his or her own representation.

How you choose to coordinate the efforts of those who represent you is not something we can answer very simply in this book, but if multiple representation is the case, then we strongly suggest detailed discussions among all parties concerned and documentation of those communications.

Publisher complications can arise if both collaborators are already under contract to write other books individually for different publishers. If there is any overlap in the types of books, or if there are options on the individual's contracts with the publishing house, then the prior contractual responsibilities need to be thoroughly examined at this point and adjustments made. This is where the help of an attorney or a literary agent can be so valuable in clarifying the obligations of both parties.

- Credit

Seeing our name on the cover of a book. Having the pleasure of fans recognizing our name and immediately downloading and rushing to buy the next release. Walking by a window display of the corner bookstore and seeing...

CUT! Cut the action. No good. Take Two. We need to go back and study this scene in a little more detail.

A number of problems immediately arise. Consider, for example, *whose* name is going on the book. Your name? Your partner's name? Will you use a pseudonym? And who has the right to the pseudonym?

When we started writing women's fiction, we were told by our publisher that we had to assume a female pseudonym. Now, Jim was perfectly happy to go along and have the books come out under Nikoo's name. But Nikoo was not about to take full credit on the cover of a book when Jim was doing half the work. So instead, we talked it out and decided to use Jim's grandmother's name as our collaborative pseudonym.

The fact that the real May McGoldrick, a very literary-minded and hardworking businesswoman, had passed away more than twenty years earlier lessened the complications. At least we didn't have to worry about Grandma getting attacked by a slew of fans in a strip mall looking for autographs. (Okay, so even our concerns were a bit optimistic.)

Then came our suspense/thriller career. Our publisher felt that our contemporary thrillers would have a different audience from those reading our May McGoldrick books. So Jan Coffey was born. Jan is an acronym for Jim And Nikoo. Coffey is Nikoo's maiden name.

And we're not done. Most recently, we created Nik James, the writer of Caleb Marlowe historical Westerns.

It's not difficult figuring out where that pen name came from. But it's clear we're both getting credit.

Are we done with coming up with new pseudonyms? Maybe not.

Depending on the type of the work, there are many ways the potential problem of credit is addressed.

In nonfiction work, the publishers tend to print everyone's name on the cover. In work-for-hire, depending on the previously agreed upon arrangements, the actual writer of the work might not get anything more than a mention on the acknowledgment page.

In fiction, you see a plethora of approaches.

Marcia Thornton Jones and Debbie Dadey use both of their names on their bestselling children's series. Shirl Henke and Carol Reynard use Shirl's name. Judith Barnard and Michael Fain, the New York Times bestselling authors, used their first names to come up with the pseudonym Judith Michael. Tony and Lori Karayianni combined their first name and modified their last name to create Tori Carrington.

We could go on for pages, listing the publication names of the writing teams we've been communicating with; there's a story behind almost every one. But to save a few of the trees in our shrinking wilderness and a few digital bytes, we'll stop right here and tell you this. Make an agreement about the credit but then be flexible. Depending on the type of fiction you write, your publisher may have totally different plans for you in the end.

- Terminating the relationship

Hey, it happens.

What if, for some reason, one of the partners decides to end the collaboration in the middle of the project. This can very well happen, and it doesn't necessarily need to be the result of hard feelings or disagreements. What if one of us simply gets too sick to continue?

With some forethought, we can address possible situations at the outset of our collaboration. If one writer can't continue, is the project dead? Have we worked out in advance some financial arrangement, so the remaining writer can pick up the project and continue? Hopefully, we never have to deal with such a scenario, but we all want to be prepared.

• Warranties

We spoke earlier of the power of the written word. What if our partner, however, decides *not* to honor the agreed-upon dates and responsibilities? What's to stop him or her from blithely ignoring the whole thing? If we have included a section in our document listing warranties or even penalties for failing to honor our agreements, then the document has teeth. We simply need to be clear about how sharp the teeth are and how deeply they can bite.

This might sound a little harsh. Our partner may, after all, be an old friend, a family member, or a significant other. Or this professional relationship may be only that ... professional.

Whatever the nature of our complete relationship might be, we each need to find and operate at our own level of comfort and security when it comes to our lives and careers. The warranty section that might be acceptable for one collaborative team might be totally inappropriate for another.

Do what feels right for you *and* your partner.

• Resolution of disputes

Right about now, you may be thinking that this is getting a bit too serious for me. As long as you've read this far, though, you may as well sort out this last step – the question of how disputes are to be resolved. Will it be in court, or will some form of arbitration be enough to resolve conflicts? If we decide that arbitration is enough, will it be binding or not?

Decide up front.

Enough said.

We are all professionals, and maintaining a productive working relationship with our writing partner is one of our ultimate goals.

Being the creative people that we are, however, emotions often play a big part in our lives. We laugh and cry, and we fight with passion. We hate and love (often in rapid succession) and say things that we never meant to say. But beyond the pain and joy of the moment, most of us would like to know that we can move on without the anguish of a broken collaboration following us for the rest of our days.

Wherever the creative road leads, we want to have the relative peace of mind of knowing we've done everything we agreed to do in our professional relationship.

Remember, the purpose of the collaborative agreement

– like a prenuptial agreement – is to head off potential problems before they occur, and to make provisions if they do occur. That's all.

Clear, documented understandings regarding what is expected of everyone involved can make for long-term stability in the collaborative partnership.

That's too long to be a catchy motto, but we believe it.

Marriage à la Modem:
The How-to of
Collaborative Writing

It's inevitable. As soon as people learn that we write together, they always ask, "How do you do it?" And conditioned (as we all are) by the get-rich-quick infomercial culture we live in, these folks are looking for simple, gimmicky, one-sentence answers. We only wish the *how-to* of collaboration could be explained that easily.

Regardless of the length of the writing *courtship*, by this point you have committed yourself to this relationship we call collaboration. So this is where the real work begins.

Part II of this book will provide a hands-on approach to the collaboration process. As collaborators who are already committed to working on a project, we now need to consider more fully such specifics as routines, division of labor, and the forging of a style that is distinctly *ours*.

Before we begin, we want to keep in mind the term 'evolution.' Collaboration is a process of continual change. Change is going to be a part of how we work together as partners, and we must be mentally prepared for that. Even the pattern of our work days and the hours we spend working at our craft will require flexibility.

Because of this, we constantly find ourselves revisiting the basics of our communication skills and we will do this in the following chapters. Just as professional baseball players constantly practice and polish the basics skills they learned as Little Leaguers, we too must practice and polish and refine our own relationship skills.

Our later chapters will address the revision process and deal specifically with methods for sharpening those essential tools for collaborative revision; namely, techniques for underhanded negotiation and blackmail.

Once we have mastered writing *the book* and have finished the first project, then we need to regroup and decide where exactly we want to go with these newfound skills. We'll finish with a chapter on promotion, since there's not much point in telling a story if nobody's going to hear it.

As we roll up our sleeves and dig in, we will start by sharing with you techniques for combining your talents, as well as some stories regarding routines, writing, and methods of forging a style – that third voice that ultimately takes over.

Hopefully, by reading about some other teams' experiences – and their mistakes – we can find a technique that works best for us.

6

After the Honeymoon
OR, LEARNING TO LIVE TOGETHER

HONEYMOON. What a lovely term! The very word conjures up images of a month cruising the sparkling waters of the Mediterranean or cuddling in gondolas in the canals of Venice beneath a warm, golden moon. When two people commit to one another, it represents that stress-free ... well, relatively stress-free period when we are really learning about one another and shaping the nature of the budding relationship.

Let's stop right there. Never mind Venice or the smooth waters of the Mediterranean. If, at any moment during your collaborative journey to this point, you have felt a twinge of stress or even a slight disagreement, then we strongly suggest that you don your helmet, put on the life preserver, and buckle your seat belt, because this stage in the process has the potential for a full nine-point-five on the Richter scale with a forty-foot tsunami to match.

So how are we going to deal with stress and disagreement?

Actually, we are *not* recommending helmets, life

preservers, or seat belts. Just the opposite. We believe the most appropriate action – at the risk of sounding *pollyan-naish* – is for each of us to peel off the defensive armor and lighten up. This is the most effective means of self-defense that we know.

Communicate (and protect your relationship) through humor.

What is the most ridiculous film you have ever seen?

What is the one quote that always brings a smile to your lips?

What single moment can you recall that will always cheer you up, even momentarily?

Pin up that photograph of Rhett and Scarlet. Or Butch and Sundance. Or Thelma and Louise. Type out that quote and hang it up. Consider surrounding yourself with things that you know will conjure a favored moment.

For the longest time, Nikoo had a drawing hanging over her computer – a drawing that our elder son drew when he was in second grade. It's a crayon depiction of a pirate ship attacking a castle perched on a high bluff. At the helm of the ship, the pirate captain has a sword pointed threateningly in the direction of the surrendering owner of the castle. The pirate is marked 'Mommy' and the besieged landlubber is marked 'Papa.' One long look at this brightens her mood under the worst of conditions.

Jim, however, is more into quantity. If there is an inch left on the wall of his office, then there is room to hang up another painting or drawings. If there is any space on the floor, then there is room for a couple more of his favorite books.

Like a virus, a sour mood can be contagious, damaging, and counterproductive in the work environment. Often, even though we know this, we *allow* ourselves to be childish and self-indulgent, making everyone around us miserable too. We simply don't take the time to consider those things that might steer us into a more productive frame of mind.

And that's not even the worst of it. Sometimes we actively seek out confrontations. As collaborative writers, it's easy enough to call our partner, or even march downstairs. All of us have stylistic quirks that can be used as tinder. If we're itching for a fight, it won't take two hours of discussing the story to make us both feel the hives popping out on our skin and our blood pressure soaring to stroke levels. We can do that in two minutes if we really put our minds to it.

But that is no way to write a book. We just can't give into this kind of unprofessional behavior.

Lynn Kerstan's advice?

Keep your sense of humor. Especially, be ready to laugh at your own failings. Discovering and acknowledging our own weaknesses before our partner does is *always* safer.

When we actively add some humor to a work relationship that has potentially adversarial moments built into it, we are often surprised at how much easier everything flows.

Oh, and from experience we can say that it is always recommended that you laugh at yourself first, *before* you laugh at your partner.

Nikoo admits she should be reported to the Department of Grammar Protection for being a chronic comma abuser.

Jim openly agrees that he has been in therapy (and may need medication) to help combat MBS, known to lay personnel as the Missing 'Be' Syndrome. His long held claims that a computer virus must have been deleting the word 'be' from his prose simply could not [be] believed after anti-virus software became standard.

And this is just the start of it.

Jim regularly makes scenes too violent for Nikoo's liking. Nikoo tends to ramble on, continuing a scene pages after all reason for continuing has been eliminated and the characters have gone home and retired for the night.

We each know our failings, but still, when it comes to our own writing – whether the cause be temporary amnesia or the more common lapse in sanity – we forget. So it's up to our partner to remind us – gently, with good humor – of our shortcomings.

Jim, there are more heads rolling around in the dirt than there are bodies. You do recall that we are writing *romance*, and not a script for *Halloween XXXXIII*?

Nikoo, I loved that punch-line that you wrote to finish the chapter *three pages ago*. Do you think we should put it ... ahhh, somewhere near the *end* of the chapter?

We are not born comedians, but we've been learning to cultivate what we've got since we started writing together. You could do the same.

Establish goals

Naturally, we all have one ultimate goal in mind – to write a one-hundred to five-hundred page manuscript with our partner without bloodshed, hard feelings, or a threat of lawsuit.

Sounds good so far. But wait, let's push this ultimate goal business a little further.

Because we're old-timers, the following represents our early imaginings.

The manuscript is ready for mailing (yes, we used to do this), and we tuck it under an arm and cross the street to the post office.

Suddenly, out of nowhere, a limousine careens around the corner. We try to dive to safety, but one spiked high heel (Jim *always* dresses formally when he goes to the post office) is firmly wedged in storm drain. Yanking it free as the limo bears down on us, we slip in a puddle and land squarely on our dignity, our manuscript just beyond the reach of our outstretched fingers.

The limo, narrowly missing us, obliterates Jim's spiked high heel and screeches to a halt. The back door of the car flies open and there, like some modern-day Rochester of Thornfield Hall, Steven Spielberg steps out.

We are unable to utter a word, and everyone naturally assumes that we've suffered a concussion. As the emergency crew whisks us to the hospital, we see Mr. Spielberg pick up the manuscript from the street.

When he contacts our partner with the news of the accident, our collaborator – savvy business person that she is – manages to pitch the work, and by the time we

leave the hospital thirty minutes later, our partner and
agent have already concluded that multi-million dollar
deal with options for....

Well, even if the ultimate goal varies a little from writer
to writer, we all probably have some fantasy of what
success might entail. Therefore, we need to get back to that
tiny little detail of *what we need to do* to get that finished
manuscript ready.

Lynne Snead and Joyce Wycoff, in their work on
creative collaboration, note that some people "think and
speak their ideas rapidly while others need time to reflect
and develop their ideas."

To avoid losing anything, we mentioned before that we
use a notebook. If we're talking or brainstorming, one of
us will take notes. If we're thinking individually about the
work, we will record our thoughts.

We use the notebook not only because the two of us
are different in our approach to idea development, but
because it provides a tool for establishing our goals for the
day, for the week, or for the length of the project.

When we start work on a novel, we establish a goal of
writing a thousand words a day.

Picking a word goal can be good or bad. It's good
because it gives us some sense of pace for our production.
It forces us to sit at the computer every day and – good or
bad or indifferent – continue to write.

Sometimes, we have the ability to write twice that
amount, or three times or more. On a day like that, it's
easy to rationalize stopping at around a thousand words.
After all, we have accomplished our *quota* for the day. In
our brain we've shifted from *goal* to *quota*. It's important to
keep in mind our ultimate goal. We need to see that word
count (or number of minutes or pages) as a first-down

marker and not the end zone. If we can do that, more often than not we'll push on.

After more than two decades of writing, the reality of our collaboration is that we *need* the daily goals, the daily drive. Each novel needs its own time to percolate before the writing takes off. The thousand words a day is just that. It's a period for us to get to know the story and our characters. Once we settle in and feel at home with the project, the words accumulate at a faster and faster rate. On every single project – that's more than four dozen novels – we started with a daily goal of a thousand words a day. And with every novel, we finished up writing three to five thousand words a day or more.

Establish routines

If you think devising a set schedule to write is difficult for one person, then perhaps you think it might be horrendous for two. The secret is to be flexible and to change the routine as the need arises.

> Our overall process changes from book to book. Usually, while I'm working on another project, Mary will come up with an idea, run it by me for my input, then get on with plotting and research. Nothing's ever set in concrete. No two books follow quite the same procedure.
> – Bronwyn Williams

In addition to writing with her sister Mary Williams as Bronwyn Williams, Dixie Browning has written many novels on her own. Talented and prolific as they are, their routine reinforces the idea that we need to use whatever works for us.

Others need a more regular routine, as Bernice Picard told us:

> We both work at other jobs, so we make an appointment to meet at least once a week. Some days I arrive early so we can do dinner and socialize before getting down to work.

The mother and daughter writing team of Leslie-Christine Megahey and Shirley Holden-Ferdinand (AKA Christine Holden) have a routine of meeting for morning coffee to discuss their progress on the work. A set time and a set place on a set schedule. The very consistency of it lends itself to structure and steady productivity.

Other teams, such as Cynthia Serra and Beth Ciotta, choose contact that is less frequent than daily meetings over coffee:

> When we're at the threshold of a new story, Beth and I get together for a weekend and hash out plot, characters, motivations, goals, etc. By the end of the weekend, we're clear as to where to start the story, and then we decide where each of us will begin.

Many writers believe that this routine of intense discussion at the beginning of a project – similar in some respects to the idea of the *book in a week* technique being used by a number of successful writers these days – may do wonders for your creativity and productivity. And truthfully, no matter how many hours a day you talk on the phone with your partner, sometimes there is no substitute for sitting side by side, where there is no escape from getting the work done.

We adhere to a regimented work schedule, working five days a week, eight or nine hours a day. At the end of each session, we discuss the next two or three scenes and decide who will write each. If either has difficulty with their scene, we may write it together, paragraph by paragraph.

By 9:00 AM each morning, we are at our computers, writing the scenes. When we finish a scene, we email it, then the receiving partner cuts and pastes it to the respective chapter.

Over the phone, we then read the scene aloud, editing and making additions or deletions until we are both happy with the outcome. Those times when a scene doesn't seem to make it, we rethink and rewrite it. Sometimes we just throw it out.

After completing a chapter, we go over it individually at night. The next day, we discuss the chapter, make the changes, add depth, and insert crucial details that one may have forgotten.

Writing with a partner is like backing up a computer; what one of us forgets, the other remembers.

– Louie Dillon and JB Hamilton Queen

This technique of working together that Louie and JB devised is an admirable one. Ideally, this is what we might strive for in our routine. Eight or nine hours a day, five days a week. But then, life has a way of dictating how many days or hours we *do* have each week. Lisa Barnett told us,

Melissa especially has a strong daily routine; mine is more haphazard, depending upon my work schedule, when I'm traveling, etc.. But I try to work for a couple of hours every evening, which sometimes means several pages, sometimes a few paragraphs, depending on how the words are coming.

Lori & Tony Karayianni (AKA Tori Carrington), on the other hand, had a very regular routine that allowed them to maintain the lifestyle that worked for them:

Since we fit siestas into our day (a must!), we divide our work hours from 8:00 AM to 1:00 PM., then we come back again from 7:00 PM until 11:00 PM.

On Monday, Wednesday, and Friday, these hours are dedicated completely to writing. On Tuesday, Thursday, and Saturday, we write in the morning, then see to the other duties in the evening, or sneak in a few hours off.

We are all creatures of habit, to some extent. We shouldn't try to be something we're not. In devising a collaborative writing routine, we should take into consideration the work habits that we've found we're most comfortable with, the work habits that we've found to be the most successful for us.

We wrote our first three books between the hours of 8:00 PM and midnight, writing seven days a week. With two sons and day jobs, we had to. That routine worked fine for that period of time in our life.

After that, we moved to a regimen that was less structured but more conducive to the joys and the requirements of family life. We called this, writing what you can, whenever you can. With the help of a laptop and a set of ear plugs to block background noises, it's amazing how productive ten minutes here and a half hour there can be. Yes, we were the ones working in the car while the violin lesson was taking place.

Now that our sons are adults and out of the house, we still maintain a routine. These days, we work seven days a week from nine to three, holidays and visits from family excluded. And our dog has a better sense of time than any clock. Three o'clock is feeding time. The work day is over.

The bottom line? Establish a routine that works for each of you, but make it flexible.

Forge your own collaborative process

Writing. It all comes down to this. The actual writing of the prose that will eventually be a novel. Just as there are a multitude of audiences and genres and manuscript requirements out there, there are a number of ways that individual writing teams get the work done. In this section we have tried to gather a sampling of other teams' experiences and secrets and strategies for writing together.

When we're ready to take on a new project, one or the other of us will toss an idea into the think tank. Either something completely new, or something we've previously discussed but shelved until later.

We'll then brainstorm for hours, sometimes for days, until we're both sure this idea is the one. Then we'll jointly sketch an outline of the characters, and discuss the main plot points. Tony then takes over, applying his considerable plotting skills to map out the book – chapter by chapter, scene by scene. Once this is done, I further flesh out the characters, then set about getting the rough draft down.

Of course, nothing is ever written in stone. Quite frequently, during either the plotting or the writing, we'll hit a wall. It's then that we'll backtrack to figure out what happened. We'll sometimes take a completely different path than we originally planned. You know, like when the characters completely balk at something you had mapped out for them and refuse to cooperate. Or when a fresher course grabs us by the...well, grabs us.

Then we'll swap material. Tony will take the rough draft and strengthen weak spots, lengthen dialogue, etc., while I take his detailed outline and beat it into synopsis shape. We usually go through four turnovers before we're both satisfied with the material.

– Lori & Tony Karayianni (AKA Tori Carrington)

Lori's and Tony's method of revision involves passing the material back and forth. In that process, we see clearly defined roles. Roles that must have been established as a result of their individual talents and strengths and preferences. These are people who have done their homework up front in finding the "write" partner. Of course, being together for more than fifteen years probably helped them to know what each can contribute, but writing together *always* reveals something new about those people you may know very well in other situations.

Nonetheless, when it comes to writing that novel, we should all be very conscious of divvying up the work based on our respective talents and interests.

Amy Ingram's ten steps of writing a novel with her partner is useful for a number of reasons, offering concrete technical suggestions while remaining less specific than Tori Carrington regarding who does what in the project:

1) Idea hit. Play 'what if' game with partner to expand on idea. Map out possible plot.
2) Create character charts.
3) Create a casual schedule of who is writing what chapter, with a time period specifying when this work will be done.

4) Begin research, enough to keep the story going. (We research together and separately, then compare notes.)

5) Communicate on a daily or at least weekly basis to update each other on the progress. (In our case, we live in two different states. We call and email each other weekly updates of what we are working on.)

6) Write it.

7) Edit it separately, but incorporate the first set of changes together.

8) Re-read and edit separately, looking up the remainder of those historical facts we've been too lazy to check before.

9) Meet to read aloud the completed novel. Discuss thoughts with each other.

10) Make final edits together, creating a cover letter, and sending the manuscript off to a publisher.

In the case of compatible partners who share the same interests but don't have any strong inclinations or preferences about creating a certain aspect of the fiction, Amy's ten steps are certainly a workable arrangement. In fact, for the people we mentioned at the beginning of this chapter – the ones who want a quick step-by-step response on how to write with someone else – Amy's list is an excellent one.

But just like every complex relationship involving human beings, collaboration requires constant revision and fine tuning. Our partners and the people around us always add their little complications.

> Writing as a team has been a learning experience – doing it one way, then another, then finally arriving at the method that works best for us.
>
> When we first began, we sat side by side, writing until we agreed on each sentence. Talk about

disagreements. That first novel was probably rewritten ten times.

Thanks to the computers and phones that bridge the six-mile distance between our homes, we now can make faces and roll our eyes without the other seeing, and therefore, we get twice the work done.

– Louie Dillon and JB Hamilton Queen

Our own initial approach involved writing side by side, as well. But unlike Louie and JB, who write in different locations, unable to see the other's frustrations and facial gestures, Jim and I continue to witness one another's looks of horror and amusement and delight.

In the process we continue to cultivate our sense of humor and satiric language and even have fun with it. Of course, Jim still likes to tell stories about how, whenever it was his turn to type, Nikoo would sit on a chair next to him and stick her toes under his buttocks. And if he wrote something she didn't like...

The truth of it is that Nikoo liked to sit next to Jim with her finger on the *delete* button. She could wipe out words much faster than he could type them. Who said writing with a partner takes half the time of someone writing alone?

Since those first days, we've either worked across the room (an exceptionally large room) from each other or in separate offices. Pretty much, the only time we work side by side now is during the read through and editing. And Nikoo still keeps her finger on the delete button.

We sit side by side in front of one computer to write. We read out loud what we've written, to hear the flow and the rhythm of the dialogue. Every so often we ask, "Would this character really do this? What do they do

next?" etc.. We try to write ten hours a week. We write
(or take care of book-related business) on our lunch
breaks as well as one evening and one weekend day each
week.

   – Shelley Mosley and Deborah Mazoyer (AKA
Deborah Shelley)

This method of sitting side by side, when geographi-
cally and physically possible, appears to be the preferred
initial method for a lot of writing teams. When we started
our collaboration, we had confidence that we knew our
individual strengths and weaknesses. Even so, it took two
of us to muster the confidence to pursue the task that we
had laid out for ourselves.

Sure, we'd set out to write individually before. But
never had we started a project with the determination that
we had *writing together*. Sitting side by side, we knew that our
story would be better than anything we could write
separately.

Working that way, we offered and received immediate
critical response and feedback. We knew that every page
we completed was good enough to pass the scrutiny of a
very critical eye because our partner's name was on this, as
well. This was a confidence booster, if nothing else.

We've done things differently with different works. For
our children's book, we had a complete outline. Each
of us would write one section each week, and we
would revise when we met. This method worked well.
By the end, you really couldn't tell who had written
what.

   Now, with our adult mystery, we tend to write
"together," by which I mean one at the keyboard and the
other serving as back seat driver. This is not a good idea,

> as it confines the writing process to just those hours
> when we meet.
>
> – Lee Rouland

What Lee refers to here about the writing process being confined by a limited number of hours was a deciding factor for *us* to move away from writing side by side. In fact, with children and family and other life activities, we found ourselves shifting toward a method of taking turns. Jim would write for four hours while Nikoo held the family together for him, then Nikoo would write for four hours while Jim tried to keep catastrophe from completely wiping out life as we know it on this planet. Hey, our boys were energetic.

Still though, interestingly enough, whenever we were truly stuck on a scene – or when, after a few back and forth revisions, we found ourselves at odds – we would revert back to sitting side by side. It's amazing, but it always worked. The problem always got resolved. And that strategy continues to this day.

Some teams know that they are better off working separately. As Lisa Barnett says, "we would be miserable trying to write together in the same room." Her partner, Melissa Scott describes their routine:

> Generally, we rough out an idea verbally over a period of anything from a month to a year. Long road trips are great for this. Then I do a detailed outline. We write a very rough and often incomplete first draft by each of us picking the scenes we find most compelling and sketching them, and then one of us – usually Lisa – goes over it to create a complete 2nd draft. I go over that, and then we both work on the final draft. That's in the ideal world.

Lea Tassie told us that taking a specific character's point-of-view and writing alternating scenes is the method that worked for her and Kathleen Webb.

> For us, the novel has two points-of-view: hero and heroine. I wrote all the scenes from the hero's point of view, and Kathleen wrote all the scenes from the heroine's point of view. She kicked off with the first scene and gave it to me, and I wrote the second scene, returning the document to her for the third scene, and so on. As we were writing, we also edited each other's work.

When the collaborators use this technique, the hero and heroine obviously each have their own voice, and the styles of the two writers successfully merge.

Interesting enough, most people assume this is our style of dividing the work. That is, Jim writing the male's point of view and Nikoo writing the female's. Well, it's not.

Marcia Thornton Jones and Debbie Dadey use what they call the "hot potato" method of writing their popular children's series. "One of us does the outline and writes a couple of chapters, then emails it to the other. Books take two weeks to two years to write."

These two successful collaborators live a considerable distance apart, and their method appears to offer a workable arrangement for partners working under similar conditions.

David Nickle also writes with partners who are often located at a distance, and he sent us this:

> The method differs depending on the collaboration. With the short story "The Toy Mill," we actually began writing alternating sentences in the opening scene. Eventually, we settled on writing alternating scenes. We

didn't have much of an outline (which meant major revisions before it was ready to sell), so we tended to concentrate on over-the-top language and comedy in the first draft.

The novel was very different. We wrote the original draft as an entry into the Three Day Novel Writing Contest. According to the rules, you're allowed a one-page outline before you start, and that's what we did: ten chapters in which we more or less knew what was going on.

We made sure to stream the plot through two point-of-view characters, and alternate that point of view chapter by chapter. So we were able to write alternating chapters, more or less in parallel. We tended to keep up with one another (so Chapter One and Chapter Two would be finished at the same time, and Three and Four and so on) so both of us would be aware of any twists that had been introduced in the other's section. We did all of this in the same room working on separate computers.

By the end of the three days, we had a novel, but it was very rough, and too short for commercial publication – just 45,000 words, when an average paperback clocks in at about 80,000 words. So we let it sit awhile, and then set about expanding it at a more leisurely pace. The process for that differed dramatically; we divided the work in the same way, but tended to work from our own homes and communicate via email.

As David notes, collaborators need to be open to using a number of methods, depending on the circumstances surrounding the project and our own situation. He and his partners use everything from working side by side to writing alternating scenes to huddling together to write a novel in three days of intense combined effort.

Finished or not, the accomplishment of putting that many words on paper in such a short time – and not seriously injuring your partner in the process – is certainly remarkable.

While speed and intensity distinguish the methods that award-winning author David Nickle uses in his collaborative efforts, Alicia Rasley's technique is markedly different.

> We corresponded online. She'd write a scene and ship it to me for response and vice versa. It probably took longer that way, but we were constantly in touch and able to modify what we wrote on the basis of what the other had written.
>
> Lynn was responsible for the major plot line, and I handled the secondary love plot. If Lynn couldn't handle a scene for some reason, I'd write a draft for her to revise to suit, because she was writing so much more than I was, and this helped even it out a bit. I did the first revision, and then we passed it back and forth until we got every word right.

A clear but flexible plan, and the steady determination to produce the best possible story, appears to be a key to Lynn Kerstan and Alicia Rasley's success. Each of them already a published author of many novels, Lynn and Alicia brought their individual skills to the project, and they were determined to make the collaborative effort work. And they did.

Carol Reynard and Shirl Henke employed another interesting method of writing a novel together. After discussing the story and working out the plot problems,

Shirl would write the story longhand as Carol typed it, revising and adding details as she went.

Though the brainstorming techniques these two talented writers used varied from project to project – with one or the other conceiving the story's premise – this method of physically writing the novel remained consistent.

When it comes to collaborative writing, Judith Michael was a force. With nine *New York Times* bestsellers and millions of devoted readers around the world, this husband-and-wife team's approach to writing was something we all wanted to hear.

Before beginning to write, Judith and Michael would spend nearly a year talking about plots and characters in conversations. Once plot, subplots, characters, and locales were agreed upon (often after spirited discussions and passionate defenses of cherished ideas that a partner might not share), Judith would begin to write. Michael edited, chapter by chapter, and wrote scenarios for upcoming scenes based on their research into various professions.

After Michael's editing, Judith would do her own, rewriting whole sections, deleting others, and adding new ones in response to Michael's comments. They'd pass chapters back and forth six or more times until they were satisfied. "Or exhausted," Michael says.

Forging a style

A common complaint from people who know us well and have read our books is that they cannot tell who wrote what. Well, we actually take this as a compliment. To be honest, when we go back and read the work ourselves after a period of time, we very often can't tell, either.

Whether we've consciously crafted it or not, we all have

an individual voice. A blend of word choice, syntax, pace, and attitude, it marks the writing as the work a *particular* writer. When it comes to collaboration, the blending of these two voices may seem to be a challenging task. As a work is revised, however, a *new* voice simply emerges, as Lynn Kerstan notes:

> Always, we were conscious of blending our prose styles.
> Mine tends to be fast-paced and minimalist, while
> Alicia's is lusher and more lyrical. Each of us adjusted,
> and our editor could not tell which of us had written
> what scenes. Alicia did the final run-through, tinkering
> for style and checking for minor errors.

Even if we are not aware of it as we write the novel, the process of back-and-forth revising (perhaps six times or more in Judith Michael's case) smoothes out the style and blends the voices.

> There have been times when we've woven our thoughts
> from paragraph to paragraph, sentence to sentence,
> word to word, so tightly that even we don't know who
> wrote what anymore. It's a comfortably unorganized
> process and wonderfully inspiring.
> – Beth Ciotta

Not knowing "who wrote what" *is* the ultimate goal. This blending of voices not only creates a seamless story for the readers to read and enjoy, it also helps the reader to detach herself from the words themselves and instead lose herself in the fictional world.

We heard the story of a 16th-century Italian nun who composed music intended to adorn the religious services held in her convent. The oratorios, sung by nuns hidden behind wooden screens high in the rear of the chapel, often blended the voices of two singers in such a way that the listeners had no idea how many voices they were hearing:

> The chapel is silent. One singer begins and the other soon follows – softly at first, echoing her sister and then growing steadily stronger. Together the two performers work, their voices floating out, gradually growing louder and louder, filling the chamber. Their tones resonate off the shadowy arches, the melodic strains dividing and soaring and uniting once again. Suddenly, more singers join them, their music spiraling upward. Then, gradually, the other voices drop away until only one voice remains, finishing the piece with an articulation of harmonic patterns as intricately woven as Florentine lace. One voice. Or is it two?

Collaborative effort at its finest, and the effect achieved is one of extraordinary beauty.

As an exercise to finish this chapter, we suggest that you choose a completed passage that both you and your collaborator have had a hand in creating and writing. Try to choose a scene with one point of view. Show this piece – even better, read it aloud – to a fellow writer, a friend, or even a family member who is familiar with the work of at least one of you. Then have them write down their responses to the following questions.

1. Was the passage vivid and engaging?
2. Was it obvious what each of you wrote?

3.Where there any seams in the passage? Any awkward shifts? Noticeable changes in the style?

Weigh the responses carefully. If we blend the voices successfully in one scene or one chapter, then we can do the same throughout the entire book.

We will have discovered our collaborative voice.

7

The "Honey-Do" List
OR, LEARNING TO WORK TOGETHER

AS MANY WHO have been involved in a lengthy relationship are quick to tell us, the way we talk to our longtime partner is, for better or worse, far different from the way we communicated during the *courtship* stage. Continuing this same line of thinking with regard to our collaborative relationship, we believe that we need to focus on our goals and develop more advanced methods of communication.

In a practical sense, this chapter is a continuation of Chapter Six, since as we begin the writing and revision process, we might immediately find ourselves in dire need of some of the techniques we will suggest here. It's important to remember, as Lynne Snead notes, that collaboration enhancers – relationships, shared values, shared vision, shared creativity, and fun – actually empower you to communicate more effectively and get the job done.

Clarifying personal and professional values without a pulpit.

Creativity. Economic security. Fame. Friendship. Health. Inner harmony. Integrity. Self-respect.

Some of these, we call values. Others, we might consider to be goals. Whatever the name, clarifying "the What and Which and Who" of our creative lives is the essential first step toward the richer, fuller, and more satisfying life we are all after.

There are very few of us who have known our true calling from day one. We ourselves tried a variety of careers in totally different fields from writing. We tried anything and everything, ignoring that nagging feeling that something was missing. And then, one snowy day, we recognized the signs. We were able to identify our professional and personal goals and values. We finally knew what it was that *mattered* to us. And it was only then that we found the perfect job and the inner harmony that comes with knowing you are following the right path.

A couple of years ago, we were guest speakers at a writing conference at Columbia University in New York City. Surprisingly, the audience was comprised mainly of professionals in the fields of medicine, law, and engineering. They were there to hear Nikoo – an engineer turned writer, a left brain person successfully enjoying a right brain career.

The attendees, we learned, were mostly unhappy in their choice of careers, regardless of the monetary rewards. They were looking for a way of achieving something *more* enriching.

So how do we get there? How do we identify the goals and values that will make us happier? And is there a way to test those goals and values that we sense are so critical to our wellbeing?

Consider the "pleasant" memories. If we look back, we are certain to discover specific values that were satisfied in those *happy* occasions; thereby, helping us to identify important core values in our life.

Consider past "regrets." Whenever we sit back and say, "If I had my life to live over...", the values that are key to our existence often become more readily apparent.

We might ask, "Is that value that we've identified an absolute *value or a* should *value?"* Hunter Lewis defines an *absolute* value as a fundamental part of who we are, and therefore one we feel comfortable with. A *should* value stems from someone else's expectation of us. We may kid ourselves along for a while, but eventually we feel discomfort with this value.

We might ask, "Is the value maintaining *or* motivating?" How we choose to spend our energy clarifies the relevance of this question. Do we take actions in our life, in our career, to *maintain* what we have? Or are we *motivated* to go beyond the structures and comforts of our everyday life to get something we want but do not have?
Like all the people attending that conference in New York.

Talk versus action. Maintaining good health, for example, sounds like an important and relevant value. But do we eat right? Do we exercise even to a minimal standard? This testing of words against our daily actions is a valid gauge of what we really consider to be relevant values in our life.

Means versus ends. Anytime we identify a value as a means to achieve a different one, then the question should be raised of what matters most.

Suppose, in going through this, we could identify our top five goals and values. So why didn't we do this earlier? Why didn't we sit down and try to define what we consider to be success, putting down on paper our accomplishments and our goals, and the goals we identify as most important?

The answer is that we should have. But then, most of us don't for a good reason.

The truth is that our personal goals and our hierarchy of values change over time. What we want out of life, what we see as *success* will be different at different times. Whether it is wealth or power or fame that we seek – or positive self-image or freedom or family happiness – the importance that we place on these values will vary in the course of our lives. What is important to us at eighteen is very different from when we are thirty or fifty or seventy or ninety.

So what has all of this to do with writing with a collaborator?

Our personal values and our work – the writing – are closely linked. Successful collaborative writing requires finding the fit between our personal values and the particulars of the project we are 'partnering up' to accomplish.

Our most important values are often our key motivators; they are the source of joy when satisfied and the source of frustration when they go unsatisfied. Whether we are conscious of it or not, whether we like it or not, our values guide our everyday behavior, influence our decisions, and provide the framework for our assessment of the outcomes.

So whether we are researching the material for a story or inventing it, writing or editing, standing before a crowd and promoting our work or hiding behind a plastic planter in the corner – understanding our values and communicating that knowledge to our partner will provide a much

more productive and satisfying experience both personally
and professionally.

Victor Frankl wrote,

> Ever more people today have the means to live, but no
> meaning to live for.

Identifying our personal and professional values and
goals will clear our creative path – a path that is inherently
rocky under the best of conditions – of so many unneces-
sary obstacles.

Identifying priorities without an arbitrator.

Some of us wake up every morning and make a list.
Others prefer to live our day in a mad rush. Some of us
are truly creatures of habit. Others are born to be wild. In
Chapter Five, we shared with you how some other writing
teams set their priorities and meet their deadlines. And
when we read those stories, it becomes clear that prioritizing the different elements of writing fiction can be fertile
ground for conflict, if not out and out war.

Despite the commonly held misconception that you
can't have more than one cook in the kitchen, we *know* that
you can. As long as we take all sharp instruments away and
keep brushing up on our cooperation skills, collaboration
does work.

The first step in being able to rationally identify and
agree on priorities is to think of ourselves as a *business*.
Now, as 'Collaborators, Inc.' you can work on the key
ingredients to successful partnership.

In writing our historical fiction, we early on gave up
our individual authorial identities and became 'May

McGoldrick.' Though Jim and Nikoo McGoldrick might personally harbor a couple of bohemian souls, 'May McGoldrick, Inc.' exists because it has developed a professional framework that can be broken down into a number of definable elements:

- Goal – Our goal is to write well-researched *and* entertaining novels for a wide range of readers.
- Product – Our products are the novels that we write. And just like any other entrepreneurial business, we know that making a quality product available to our customer in a timely fashion is a key to success.
- Customers – In our case we have three tiers of customers, with the first tier being ourselves, the creative team. The second tier is the acquiring editor, and the third tier is the reading public. All have their own requirements and expectations. When we publish independently, the tiers are comprised of only ourselves and potential readers.
- Resources – We utilize a wide range of resources in running May McGoldrick, Inc.. These include everything from reference books and the Internet to research trips. We also may require, at different times, the professional services of agents, lawyers, accountants, publishing consultants, website managers, publicists, etc..

The same elements pertain to Jan Coffey, Inc. and Nik James, Inc..

· · ·

Okay, level-headed writers that we all are, we have organized our business. Now comes the time for doing a little strategic planning for success. Goals and values and skills are not the only elements that ensure success. What is our plan for achieving our goals? What is our time line? Identify those priorities – not for us as individuals, but for *Collaborators, Inc.* – and then get to work.

Advanced Communications In The Collaborative Workspace

When we first ventured into collaboration, we found ourselves constantly tiptoeing around each other's feelings when it came to critiquing the work, or even negotiating the direction of a scene.

This sure has changed. In truth, it's not that we have become callous and insensitive. Nor do we sit around, waiting for any chance to strike out at our partner.

We have, however, come to expect the highest quality we can produce...in our *joint* work. And to live up to this high expectation, we've learned to focus on the writing and to demand honesty, useful criticism, and hard work from our partner.

At this stage of our working relationship, we no longer cower and withdraw from a point of disagreement. Instead, we find ourselves becoming shrewd and calculating, particularly if there are any negotiations to be done. When it comes to communication, we have become *active* listeners.

There is a great deal at stake, so as a result we are outspoken and ready to do battle to create the best story we can. We already know that the prize is worth the sweat and the blood.

So here are some more advanced approaches.

Listening actively

No, we are not about to go over any scientific stuff about the human being's six-to-one speech-to-absorption ratio. Nor are we going to stress (again) the importance of *not* dozing off when our partner speaks. It might, however, be helpful if you go back and reread that chapter if you are getting glassy-eyed at this very moment.

Stressing the word 'actively' with regard to listening, we want to share a few hints about how to achieve a winning method of communication. Well, this is how *we* do it, anyway.

1. Make certain the atmosphere surrounding you and your partner is informal and relaxed. Don't go into any discussion with dirty dishes sitting on the table beckoning to be picked up. And turn off the TV. We don't need a news reporter in the background competing for attention. And put the phones away.

2. Repeat what your partner says. Not word for word. Just the gist of it. A paraphrase of it. As in, "Let me see if I got what you said…" This helps the discussion remain focused and on track, and sends a clear signal to your partner that what was just said actually registered.

3. Project a positive attitude and do not jump to another idea – or even offer feedback – until you are certain your partner has finished conveying what she intended to say. Force yourself to take notes, if need be.
Recalling the fact that collaborators have different personality traits, we know that this particular item can present a tough challenge for an extroverted partner when our more

introverted counterpart has the floor, having finally worked up the courage to share a few thoughts.

Very good, we've listened to what our partner had to convey and even done a bit of talking ourselves on the issue in question. The next set of advanced communication skills we need involves the potentially product-saving ability to negotiate.

Negotiating

Negotiation savvy is a very important asset in *our* communication portfolio. As we mentioned in our introduction, many moons ago we were both corporate types. We both worked for companies that took aggressive positions on the positive value of training. So when it came to negotiation skills, we were taught well.

Here we are in an intense story discussion. The trivial issues have been dismissed, and we're down to a flat out disagreement on points that are extremely important to us. What do we do?

We use every trick in the book to win our position. Body language, offers of exchange, physical threats. And of course, because of our decades long relationship, we also use every trick *not* in the book. Blackmail, favors, promises you never intend to keep.

To us, this stage of writing is business. Our ideas are valuable only if the buyer – in this case our collaborator – thinks they are valuable. And if we can't sell them to our partner, to whom do we think we will be able to sell them? It is true, we are not all born sales people. And we are not all born negotiators. We're not all born golfers either, but if you've ever been out on a golf course, you know that doesn't stop anybody.

But before we lay down our ancient and hitherto closely secrets of successful negotiation, consider Lynn Kerstan's advice:

> Don't sweat the small stuff [Hey, that would make a good title.]. No one-upmanship. When disagreements arise, make sure you really care about your position before sticking by it past the first mention. If each partner yields whenever possible, the collaboration flourishes.

If you can live with an alternative suggestion, if you think that there is a *chance* that your partner's idea might do equally well, then give it up. We are not, however, trying to make the inclination to negotiate a disagreement sound negative. By no means. But if a conflict can be resolved simply by openminded discussion, if each of us would strive not to fall in love with every word we put on paper, then we could focus our valuable time and energy on the rest of the story.

Of course, sometimes you get two obstinate extroverts like the two of us who rarely argue over the words but are more than willing to lock horns over where the second set of stairs in some imaginary sixteenth-century castle should be located. Now, talk about *important*.

Like it or not, negotiation plays a subtle part of our everyday life. We use these skills when we convince a child to wear a sweatshirt instead of a T-shirt, or coax a significant other into putting the garbage out, or persuade a certain someone that driving an extra twenty-five miles to fill up on cheaper gasoline is just not worth the time it takes to get there.

Of course, depending on our temperament, we could just let the child have his way, or take out the garbage ourselves, or go along for the ride. Whatever our temperament, sometimes we do just that, putting on a smile and making whatever compromises we need to make in order to keep some semblance of peace and harmony in our lives. Plotting all the way, of course, how to get our way *next* time.

Writing with a partner presents disagreements small and large. They come with the package. We all have, however, a lifetime of training that is ready to be put to use in refashioning the dynamics of disagreement into the productive force of creative collaboration.

First of all, shake off all the negative images of negotiation you might have. Asking for something, wanting to bargain over a scene, should not be viewed as a sign of mistrust or lack of confidence in your partner's abilities. Avoid the *doormat* syndrome. Having a doormat for a partner (or being one yourself) will not produce the best work the two of you can produce together.

In our case we've always viewed negotiation as the *least* troublesome method of settling disputes.

Remember, too, that there are five end results for all negotiations:

Win-Win.

Win-Lose.

Lose-Win.

Lose-Lose.

Walk Away.

With two collaborating writers who have so much at stake, Win-Win has to be the ultimate goal. Every other conclusion should be unsatisfactory. Hurt, disappointment, and the unavoidable breakdown in communication will forge a working relationship where creativity and productivity cannot possibly exist.

If only one of you is aware of the variety of possible

outcomes, then the responsibility falls on the cognizant individual to make certain both parties walk away satisfied with what has been settled upon.

Keep the *personal* bargaining out of your negotiating at the outset of a disagreement. You can use that approach later on to break up the tension and add humor to a discussion when stresses and strains really begin to build. Instead, try to focus on the book – the characters, revisions, whatever is driving that urge to argue.

One thing though, make sure it is the fiction that is bothering you and not the electric bill or the neighbor's dog or something else.

Lisa Barnett told us of a relevant approach she and her partner use when they reach an impasse:

> If you are really having a serious disagreement about something in the book, GO OUT TO DINNER. You have to maintain a semblance of politeness in front of the wait staff, and the 'discussion' is less likely to devolve into who didn't clean the cat's box.

In our case, we go out for walk together. One mile, two miles, five miles. As a result, our dog is the fittest animal in the neighborhood. And by the time we get back, we usually don't even recall what the problem was.

What follows is a list of hints on the type of negotiation that does not go for the *kill*, focusing instead on positive problem resolution. Don't use this list as you prepare to buy a car or even when dealing with a car warrantee tele-marketer. Save it for when you are dealing with your part-ner, that collaborator who shares your dream and passion for telling the best story possible.

Identify the story problem as well as you can, and then back off.

Don't let the disagreement escalate. In fact, sleep on it if the issue can't be immediately resolved, working on something else if you are under serious time constraints. It's amazing how different we can feel the next morning about an issue that we were ready to go to war over the day before.

Develop a coherent rationale for the change you think is important. Make it clear to your partner that your focus is on making the book better, and on nothing else.

As a matter of technique, couch your reasoning in terms that exclude the words 'I' and 'my.' In fact, as Deborah Tannen says, we should avoid using the word 'you,' as it often comes out accusingly; as in, "you always" or "you never." Try to use 'we' or 'our.'

Be ready up front to make concessions. Be flexible and understand what it is your partner is trying to achieve, regardless of what is actually happening in the fiction. Don't take the position that the exact idea that you have in your mind is the only acceptable idea. It never is, so be ready to give a little.

Stay aware at all times of your personality and your partner's personality. An introverted partner might step back from a disagreement, leading you to assume incorrectly that he is concurring with your point of view. You're heading toward a 'win-lose' outcome here, the consequences of which can be extremely damaging in the long run. And you *could* be wrong, after all.

Never resort to traditional authority positions to intimidate a partner. As mother and daughter writing team Christine

Holden wrote to us, "During writing hours, the business relationship supersedes that of the parent-child relationship. You must view each other as equals, as you would any other business associate." Negotiate fair and square, and you both will walk away from the table feeling like a winner.

Be alert to body language to understand hidden feelings in your partner during face-to-face discussions. And don't be blind to your own projections, either. We all have our own silent signs of annoyance. Tapping the fingers, rubbing the neck, crossing the legs, avoiding eye contact, getting up and seeking distance by moving across the room. Since you and your collaborator have already spent a fair amount of time talking and working together, you both are probably getting quite proficient at recognizing the signs. When you see them, adjust your approach and get immediate feedback before the defenses harden and you reach a crisis point.

Split the differences, if possible. Whatever the problem is, for the sake of finishing the story, you must set a time limit to reach an agreement. Decide that the agreement is not set in stone – that before the manuscript is finalized, you might want to revisit this section again. Then come to a mutually acceptable (albeit grudging and provisional) agreement, and move on. Be sure that neither of you walks away from the discussion feeling like a loser.

You know you've had a successful negotiation when

- both of you feel as if you've won.
- both of you agree that the negotiation was fair.
- you can embrace the (provisional) outcome.

- you would enjoy doing this again.

Of course, in spite of our promise, we've said nothing about blackmail. To be honest, this is where our own personal creativity and the nature of the relationship with our partner dictates our actions and our restraint. Or lack thereof.

Do we use that story written in high school against him? The one that sounds vaguely like a suburban *Gone With the Wind*? Or those photos we acquired from that bachelorette weekend in Vegas? Are we so driven that we should sink to this lowest of all methods of negotiation? Reduce ourselves to the level of some vile, no-good, swamp dwelling vermin?

Absolutely.

8

Maintaining the Marriage
Through Better or Worse
OR, SURVIVING THE SEVEN YEAR ITCH

THERE IS A POINT, however, when this larger picture starts to get a little fuzzy. Okay, so you've found your partner, worked out the story and the routines to get it written. You've negotiated and prioritized and composed a story that has real merit.

But if you and your collaborator are in the (at times more difficult) stage of revising that work, or if you have decided to go the traditional route and have delivered the manuscript to interested agents or editors and are now stuck in the waiting game, it's just possible that the excitement of everyday writing – the creative adrenaline high – is beginning to wear off. In its place comes a slight letdown, a hint of emotional exhaustion.

Symptoms of the letdown in this advanced leg of the journey include the doubts that begin to creep in.

Will we ever finish or sell or publish this story?
Could I have done this project alone?
Do I have the right partner?
Am I missing out on working with someone *better*?

If I stick with this partner, is there a future for us?
Do we *have* another book in us?

The purpose of this chapter is two-fold – to discuss issues inherent in collaborative revision and to help move the partners from negative thinking to a place of positive reassessment. In other words, to encourage the collaborative team to finish what they've started and see it through to the end.

Even though we may have addressed and worked out some of these issues at the beginning of the collaborative partnership, we are only human and some backsliding is inevitable. The important thing is to make the effort to move forward again.

We all need to deal with the stresses that are inherent in those moments of imminent change – moments like finishing a story – but we still have to get the creative product to readers. We still have that book to finish *completely*.

Agree in advance on the *process* of revising.

Okay, we've gotten at least the rough story down. Depending on how we work, we've either spit out the first draft in a week, or we have labored over every word, every paragraph, every scene for a year or more.

Whatever the method, the first draft is done, and we have a manuscript in hand. But we still have that grueling revision process ahead. Why grueling?

Well, there is that minor issue of combining authorial strengths. The blending of prose styles. The natural resistance to giving up our authorial identity and becoming that third, albeit stronger voice.

Come to some informal agreement ahead of time

about this stage of the work. Determine in advance who does what and who will decide that the work is done.

For example, Alicia Rasley and Lynn Kerstan agreed ahead of time that Lynn was to take the lead when it came to the major plot line, and Alicia would be in charge when it came to the revision stage.

We split the work up a little differently. In the later stage of our own revision process, Nikoo looks for inconsistencies and weaknesses in the storyline while Jim focuses on style and finish. And, as we said earlier, this is a point where we *often* sit side by side to reach agreement.

Let's back up a step. Some writers, like David Nickle and his collaborators, prefer to write fast, agreeing ahead of time that major revisions would be dealt with after the draft is completed. Other teams favor polishing as they go along.

We belong to the latter group. As Nikoo (in constant discussion with Jim) writes the rough draft, Jim follows, adding whole passages and scenes, detail, and finish. Nikoo then immediately revisits the work and *deletes* everything Jim has just done.

This method works beautifully, eliminating a lot of conflict we might have over these scenes later on. After all, what are the chances of Jim remembering *where* he placed that second set of stairs after four hundred pages.

The darn thing is that he *always* remembers.

Have a clear expectation about the process. Decide who should take the lead at this stage. You might even decide ahead of time about the timeframe that is reasonable for revision of the book.

Be honest. Be gentle.

Clear, honest, constructively worded feedback is key to productive revising with a partner.

As active volunteers in a variety of writing groups, we participate as judges in contests and as critique partners in chapter meetings. Too often, we find *glaring* flaws in a story's plot or characters in a work that has been written by a collaborative team or that has been produced with feedback from a regular critique group. How can this happen, we ask? Either the feedback is not forthright enough in the group, or it was ignored. If it was ignored, then it's possible that the reason may lie in the delivery of the advice.

Individuals join critique groups to get help creating something that is better than what they can produce alone. It's difficult to look at our own work with complete objectivity, so we seek constructive critical responses from others.

The trade-off is that we provide the same for the others in the group. If honesty and feedback – gently and constructively worded – are missing from these sessions, however, then we as critique partners have failed in accomplishing what is expected of us.

The same goes for collaborators. This final stage of writing, the revision process, is crucial to the success of the work. Here we have a final opportunity to identify the story's weaknesses, to change what must be changed, and to make it the best the two of us can produce.

Of course, all of this must take place in a reasonable period of time, for this work is only a stepping stone to the next project and the next. Learning and growing as writers is what keeps us constantly moving ahead.

Harness that creative *synergy*.

What is this 17th-century word that has been dominating the business world for the past few decades?

Pure and simple, it means the power of cooperative effort. If you plant certain plants close together, the roots commingle and actually improve the quality of the soil so that both plants will grow better than if they were grown separately. If you put two pieces of wood together, as in the laminating process, they will hold much more than the weight each could hold separately. The principle behind synergy is that the whole is greater than the sum of its parts. One plus one equals three ... or more.

Nikoo's engineering-trained left brain might disagree with the last statement, but her right brain accepts it completely.

> Clapping with the right hand
> only produces no noise.
> – Malay Proverb

> When spider webs unite,
> they can tether a lion.
> – Ethiopian Proverb

> Two heads are better than one.
> – Circus Sideshow Proverb

It is not a new concept, but we feel it in our professional and personal life. It is one of those basic truths that has become proverbial, and yet we rediscover it in our own lives all the time.

In collaborative writing, we have a partner who brings to the work another point of view and a different command of the language. They bring an additional world of experiences. They can encourage us and help us through difficult scenes.

Synergy is the principle that makes collaborative writing work.

> Collaboration doesn't work for every couple, but there is always a friend or a relative with whom one could find the similarities needed to create that synergy.
> – Kathryn Falk

> We are a collective of consciousness, thinking and writing as one.
> – Louie Dillon and JB Hamilton Queen

> I sometimes think we are like tent posts, leaning on one another.
> – Lee Rouland

> The writing we've done together is our best work to date, and, as predicted, we've become stronger writers individually. We found that our weaknesses weren't necessarily weaknesses, just underdeveloped skills waiting to be nurtured.
> – Cynthia Serra and Beth Ciotta

This gradual change comes across not only in the writing of the novel, but in the revision process, as well.

> We are both fairly thick-skinned. Our goal was to write the best darn story that we could. Neither of us took offense at the other's comments, suggestions, or red-penciling. *We truly believed each and every change enhanced the story.*
> There is no room in a collaboration for someone

who believes that every word they write is carved into
stone, someone who can't accept constructive criticism.
  – Kathleen Webb

This *power of two* goes even beyond the actual writing
and revising. It enables us to handle other aspects of the
profession: the rejection that is inherent in this business, the
feeling of not being good enough, the feeling of isolation.
  Louie Dillon and JB Hamilton Queen assert,

For either of us to write on our own would be like
stumbling around in a dark forest, lost and without
direction. As a team, we never have to face a blank page
or take rejections alone.

Having a partner, a soulmate in the writing process,
helps us in so many ways.

THE MARITAL RETREAT: OR, THE 15,000-MILE CHECKUP

We can go on for days, weeks, and months talking about
the positive joys of collaboration, ignoring issues that may
be festering just beneath the surface. Or we can try to look
hard at the relationship, analyze the process, and make
sure that latent problems – no matter how small – are
corrected for the next time around. If we are honest, we
will look for the sources of potential conflict, which can be
separated into four major areas:

Personal differences
Information problems
Role incompatibility
Environmental stress

Personal differences – misperceptions and erroneous expectations

We already know that as writers and as human beings, we are all different. But the need to communicate with our partners, to understand them, and maintain a relationship based on shared goals is a critical part of working effectively together. It is often, however, the *details* that cause the biggest problems. One writer told us of a relationship that is on hiatus at this point:

> The reason we ended our partnership had not so much to do with what we wrote as it did when and how we wrote. Our personality differences and work styles raised issues no compromise could resolve. I am a very deadline-oriented person. I like to schedule out the book, create a plan of when to have what chapters done. Even if I'm not completely happy with what I wrote, at least I kept writing and got something done.
>
> My partner is a perfectionist. She will read the work over and over again, and rewrite and rewrite until the book (or chapter) has almost come to a standstill.
>
> It drove me crazy to wait and rewrite; and it drove her crazy to rush to a conclusion. I didn't work within her schedule, and she didn't work within mine.
>
> When we found that the writing wasn't fun anymore and was hurting our friendship, we decided to call it quits. In this case, our friendship came before our business.

Frustrated as they were while going through it, the two

partners actually both emerged as winners, since they walked away from the collaboration process with their longstanding friendship intact and a few valuable lessons learned.

These two writers learned that discussing personal differences and expectations before beginning a project is more important than discussing literary style and plot. They learned a lesson about including deadlines in the collaboration agreements.

Again, this type of conflict does not need to be the end for a collaborative partnership. It can very well be merely a stepping stone as we learn how to compromise and communicate.

Information problems – deficiency and misrepresentation

At first glance, this source of conflict seems to indicate an element of malice. Sounds like "rats in the pantry," as Jim's grandfather used to say.

Perhaps, but not necessarily.

Consider this scenario:

You and your partner have published your work. Now you have an agent or an editor. You personally have been *planning* a great discussion with your editor about *another* project that the two of you are working on. You know in your soul that this next project could become an instant bestseller. You've planned out in your head, and you've decided you will not sell this new project to this particular editor unless she is willing to pay for it. Not just pay for it, you're thinking, but pay *BIG*. You've been imagining business negotiations, auctions, and bidding wars.

Then one day, your partner is on the phone with this particular editor and, unaware of any of your grand schemes, downplays the project and inadvertently buries any opportunity for that big pitch.

Conflict? Count on it. And it all boils down to miscommunication.

Surprisingly enough, recovering from such a blow is easier than remembering the next time around to speak up. It's a process that requires constant, conscious effort.

As close as the two of us are to each other, situations often occur with us in our everyday dealings with people. There have been instances where misinformation and misrepresentation of our work cause conflicts that need to be talked out and resolved.

The thing to remember is that information deficiency is something that *we* are each responsible for and that we can correct through a conscious effort to communicate fully.

Role incompatibility – differing views on goals and responsibilities

He said, she said. I said, you said.

We are not going to say that we told you so, but you *should* have drawn up an agreement ahead of time that identified your goals and stated the responsibilities of each individual.

Despite having written agreements, however – regardless of having all the documentation in the world – in the process of doing the actual writing there will undoubtedly be instances when a partner's views on what and how and when something should be done will change. Now, in most cases we can work through that, remembering that processes can evolve and that flexibility needs to be a key element in creative collaboration.

But what if this new role that your partner desires to play conflicts with your abilities? For example, what if you are not a *finish* person, and now the two of you are only interested in writing a first draft? Sadly, the answer might be that this is the last book you two write together.

But the conflict is not necessarily limited to writing. How about research? What if one partner gets tired of always being the one to do it?

Or even juicier. What if the two of you are life partners as well as writing partners, and one of you finds that the sex scenes that are being written reveal too much about a certain personal relationship?

We are not saying that the collaborative unit should be dissolved because of any of the above conflicts, but we *are* saying that it is much easier to discuss and decide on these issues before starting the *next* book.

Think of it as a flu shot. You get it when you're still healthy.

Environmental stress and distance

Your child has strep throat, so there goes a week of writing. Your computer just crashed, and you're out of commission a week. The storm of the century has just knocked out power, and there's no telling when it's coming back on. You hate your day job and everyone you work with, and depression is affecting your writing.

Whether you live in the same household as your partner, or whether that partner is a continent away, these types of pressures are very real for one and all of us. But unlike some of the other sources of conflict listed above, we can work through most of these. Understanding, flexibility, compassion, pitching in when the other needs a hand. And as we've said again and again, communicating how these pressures are affecting us is a key to working out those problems and staying productive.

Distance deserves some attention here. Lack of communication and coordination of effort can be sources of conflict for long distance collaborators, but the same kind of problems can surface when you're working in separate rooms.

Not long ago, we were each writing a sequence where one scene was to lead immediately into the next. After talking out the action of both scenes, we went to the computers. When we switched places a few hours later, Nikoo's scene referred to a beautiful, sunny spring day, while Jim's depicted a wild, dark, and stormy afternoon. Changeable weather in them Highlands. And in the workroom.

Okay, so we've identified various categories and specifics on conflicts that you might have experienced in the course of completing that project. Now what do we do with it?

Let's think of it along the lines of taking that not-so-new car to the mechanic after the initial 15,000 miles. Jim drops off the car and asks the mechanic to do whatever needs to be done. He does not ask for an estimate. Nikoo picks up the car later and receives a detailed bill that includes parts and labor. Although she is a bit price-shocked, she does not immediately consider the possibility of sending the car back to the manufacturer as a lemon. The performance of the car so far has been satisfactory, and this checkup was only for the purpose of evaluation. And yes, to adjust whatever needed adjusting after Jim's little off-road adventure through a cornfield one particularly foggy night.

If you understand everything that was said, please continue. If not, you can email Nikoo for a more detailed lesson in dealing with pricey automobile mechanics and unruly husbands.

Nonetheless, just keep in mind that even the most productive, well-oiled machines occasionally need a checkup and service.

Get to the *US* stage.

Abraham Maslow identified, in his famous hierarchy of needs, the individual's need for belonging – for affiliation and companionship and even friendship. With everyone we interviewed for this book, the familiar words kept coming back to us. Friends. Good friends.

In some cases, the collaborators didn't start that way, but in the process of working together, two individuals invariably became friends, a team, an *us*.

Even if you live in the same household and have been together for decades, even if you are two thousand miles apart and electronically pass your work back and forth, whatever the arrangement, writing together establishes the foundation for forming that *us* relationship. It is, however, a relationship that needs to be consciously nurtured. Lynn Kerstan gave us a list of suggestions for preserving and developing this valuable new entity:

- Be lavish with sincere praise. Writers need reassurance, and collaborators should reinforce each other when confidence falters.
- Don't let grievances smolder, enduring them in silence. With tact, address perceived problems before they build up into major problems.
- Devise a way of working together that plays to each writer's strengths.
- Never 'bad-mouth' your partner to others.
- At all times, be professional. A writing collaboration should be conducted as a

> business, however close the personal
> relationship.
> • Keep your sense of humor.

The *seven-year itch* does not need to end a long-term relationship. It simply represents a moment of change that needs to be dealt with consciously and honestly. With a renewed focus on the benefits that exist in maintaining a relationship built on shared goals – a relationship that meets the needs of the individuals as well as the team – the itch will not develop into any condition fatal to the partnership.

Dealing successfully with this stage can result in a stronger, more mature relationship that carries us forward into more creative and productive realms.

9

The Second Honeymoon

How sweet the moonlight sleeps upon this bank!
Here will we sit, and let the sounds of music
Creep in our ears. Soft stillness and the night
Become the touches of sweet harmony.
Sit, Jessica. Look how the floor of heaven
Is thick inlaid with patens of bright gold.
There's not the smallest orb which thou behold'st
But in his motion like an angel sings...
— William Shakespeare

CELESTIAL HARMONY, recognized and admired and envied by humans from the time we first thought to turn our gaze upward.

And here on earth, we constantly strive to bring those "touches of sweet harmony" into our lives, into our relationships. Sometimes, we even achieve periods of success in that endeavor. But harmony does not come about in the collaborative relationship without effort. We soar when the relationship is working, and we plummet earthward when it doesn't. When it works, it is a magical thing. Lisa Barnett told us,

> It's great working with a collaborator; I create a character, and it's thrilling to see what Melissa can do with that character, which gives me something additional to springboard off.

We agree.

The second honeymoon represents an advanced stage in the collaborative relationship, a period where a level of insight has evolved, where we can build on and improve the productivity of the creative partnership.

Unlike life, which we experience only once (as far as we know), collaboration is something that we are able to experience again and again. We can learn from our mistakes and strive for improvement. At the completion of a project, we can draw back, contemplate the dynamics of the process, and try it again if we like. In fact, each time through, we ourselves find that we have a better map of the peaks and valleys facing us.

We definitely do sit back and assess where we are after every project. For some partnerships, we have to admit, the view is not very pretty, but at least *knowing* allows for corrective *action*.

Growing apart. Growing together.
Learning to love change.

Collaborations that are complete *lemons* are few and far between. After all, we considered carefully before committing, didn't we? But each collaborative experience brings its own challenges and rewards and lessons.

David Nickle, who has collaborated with different people on various projects, tells us that he invariably takes what he's learned from one collaboration into the next. In short, nothing you learn in a collaboration is a waste of time.

Others, like Lynn Kerstan and Alicia Rasley, started their collaboration with only one book in mind. What they learned has been invaluable for them:

> We were always primarily independent writers with projects of our own and never intended the partnership to be ongoing. One day we may collaborate again, but the process is enormously time-consuming. Perhaps when we are independently wealthy.

Then there are others like Lea Tassie and Kathleen Webb who have not dissolved their team but have had to put it on hold due to other commitments. Lea told us,

> If two writers have different strengths and weaknesses, collaborating will produce a stronger book. This happened with Kathleen and me – her strong imagination and storytelling abilities complemented my skill in organization and language. And, while we are not working together at the moment, we've developed a friendship that promises to last a lifetime.

The key for many writers may be to think of each project as its own entity. That way, we are able to grow apart and still get back together when we're ready, when we have a project that calls for the combined talents of two writers.

But then, of course, there are other collaborators, like us, who love change *within the relationship* and try to implement each change in the improving *us*. We long ago discarded thoughts of growing apart. We're actually having fun working at growing together.

So whatever your first experience with collaboration, think of it as one step in that upward spiral of experience. Just keep moving.

Regrouping. Setting new rules.

Think change.

This single statement has been a big part of the answer that we have been giving to writers who are considering taking a stab at collaboration. Growing, modifying, continuously reassessing and regrouping have been a big part of our own experience.

Fortunately, no matter how difficult the going was while we were writing a story, we've never pulled up short after completing it and said, "*Never* again." Each time, after reassessing the sources of conflict and considering how we could improve upon the process for the next project, we have always focused our sights ahead. Always forward.

There has rarely been a thought of *me* when it comes to writing; instead, we've each focused on *us*.

Louie Dillon and JB Hamilton Queen have approached change and growth in a very similar fashion. Their advice?

List the problems you and your partner encountered during your first try at collaborating. After defining the problem, between the two of you generate alternate solutions with the focus on building on the other's ideas. Try to come up with a long-term alternative.

Collaborating is that total commitment, that burning desire, and tenaciousness must be there in both partners.

Similar to any marriage or any long-term commitment, Louie and JB believe and practice togetherness in their writing every day. For them, growing apart has never been an option they'd wanted to consider. But despite the fact that their advice is universal for all writing partners, their form of collaboration is not feasible for everyone. Not all of us have that talented sibling or spouse or significant other who matches our own "burning desire" when it comes to storytelling.

After two successful collaborations with two different authors, David Nickle shared this advice with us:

- Don't collaborate on a story or project to which you've got a strong emotional attachment – because you're going to have to give up a lot of control if you're going to collaborate fairly. Collaborative works should be projects that intrigue you as an individual writer, but don't consume you ... yet.
- Pick a collaborator whose work you respect and enjoy, and who shares as many of your own ideas about fiction or journalism or whatever it is you're writing, as possible.
- You've got to be able to meld your styles seamlessly, and that means your styles have to be, if not identical, close enough so as not to matter. With that much said, it is good to pick someone whose strengths complement your own. But in a good collaboration, you shouldn't be able to tell who wrote what.

Amy Ingram also sent us a list of "do's and don'ts" that she has learned about the collaboration process.

- Do find a partner who is *like you*. He or she doesn't necessarily have to write like you, but they should share some common values, principles, and work habits.
- Do establish who will be the spokesmen or *point person* for the team. For example, who will do most of the talking at conferences and with editors and agents, if you decide to go for traditional publication? It's important to have one person relay a consistent message and a personality that can easily be recalled. But both people must agree on what the spokesman is saying.
- Do break down the responsibilities.
- Do be willing to compromise.
- Do listen clearly to and explore your partner's ideas. If she feels like you're open to her ideas; she'll be more open to yours.
- Do communicate with your partner. Don't take off in a direction that may change the course of the story without consulting with the partner.
- Do create a contract before publishing.
- Do map out a plan of who is doing what and when, and follow the schedule.
- Do your share of the work and stay within the schedule. It's only fair, if you expect to get at least half of the revenue.
- Don't sacrifice friendship over a business dispute.

With the exception of delegating a spokesperson,

Amy's list alludes to circumstances that many other collaborative teams have encountered, as well. The idea of picking one individual to speak for the two, however, is a decision that depends on the individual abilities of the writing team. We like to think of the team May McGoldrick, Jan Coffey, or Nik James as one body with two heads. Actually, with two very talkative heads.

Look at the personality traits and verbal abilities and preferences of your own writing team. You are the only ones who can decide which is the right way to go. And whatever your decision, *that* is the perfect choice. Trust your judgment.

You've learned to walk. Prepare to run.

Wouldn't life be so much easier if we could live our lives over again with that treasure of knowledge we've acquired this time around. Just think about skipping all that Pre-algebra and Geometry and Calculus and diving right into Differential Equations. Think of what fun it would be taking Fluid Dynamics and Fracture Mechanics again.

Hold it right there, Nikoo. Your left brain took charge for a moment.

We wrote our first novel in nine months. The second one was finished in six months. The third in three months. Following the same pattern, we wrote our fourth novel in one day. You don't believe it?

You're right. We didn't.

It took us a little over nine months. But the truth still remains that we were barely three quarters of the way through one project when we were already starting to think about the next. And, perhaps because of that, we've found that working on the next story is always easier than working on the last.

We all – well, most of us – strive for some level of physical fitness. In our case, we focus more on mental fitness, creative fitness, writing fitness. And just as you cannot run a marathon tomorrow unless you've been in training, we believe the same holds for writing.

The inspiration to write – the *Muse* some might call it – is a trainable being. Keep her exercising. Keep her in shape even between projects. So you've finished a book and accomplished what you set out to do. Great. How long of a breather do you need? Put those running shoes back on and, however you can, get back on the course. You have, right now, the training and stamina that will help you to stay in that marathon.

One life. One race. This is not a warm-up.

———————

Louie Dillon and JB Hamilton Queen, and Dixie Browning and Mary Williams are two teams of sisters who sent us their comments regarding collaboration. Though each of these sets of partners work in a different fashion, we found it interesting that their work relationships contain many similarities.

Each group speaks very eloquently about such defining attributes as the boundless respect and the trust that each partner has for the other with regard to both talents and contributions. They each speak about the humor and the acceptance they have in viewing each other's shortcomings.

Although we all know that this type of collaboration is extraordinary, all things considered, we thought it appropriate to share what Louie Dillon and JB Hamilton Queen told us about their relationship. Second honeymoon? This is about the most solid of collaborative relationships:

> Collaboration for us is like a well-worn shoe, but for others that shoe may be too tight and cause blisters. We feel that our personal and writing relationships are extremely rare. We love and understand each other, have been together all our lives, and plan to write as many novels as we have years left...collaborating.

10

The Family Portrait
OR, PROMOTION

EVER NOTICED how the family portrait has changed over time?

We have one of Jim and his siblings, all dressed up in their Sunday best. Three younger kids sitting on a studio bench with the two oldest standing behind them. The backdrop is plain white. The photo is sepia colored.

Skip down a few decades. Living room walls are often adorned with similar portraits – families lined up, but now sitting and standing in more casual clothing. The backdrop is blue or mauve or whatever the local department store was offering.

Nowadays, the family portrait is a snapshot taken on your phone.

In short, styles and approaches change.

Promotion, the portrait you hope will attract a reader to you and your books, has also evolved. But whereas before, it took decades for something new to come about, now it's a matter of days.

When you research this aspect of the writing business, you hear about approaches that are successful in reaching readers today. But it is almost a guarantee that they will give way to something else tomorrow. What seemed like solid ground months or a year ago is now often little more than monetary quicksand.

That sounds a little negative, but it actually isn't. These are opportunities. There are always new ways to promote yourselves and your work. You just need to stay on top of it. And here is where having a partner – one with whom you can divide knowledge and promotional work hours and budget – is priceless.

You've written a fantastic book, now let's give it an extra push and get it into readers' hands.

A disclaimer first – when it comes to promotion, any published book is obsolete before the author hits the distribute button. Still, we'd like to share a few things that might help.

PROMOTION BASICS

Prepublication

The earlier you get started on promoting the release of your work, the better prepared you'll be. Most distributors and publishers plan for books to be displayed in their catalogues up to a year in advance. And these retailers count preorders on release day. These early sales can land an author on a bestseller list after the book's first week on sale, whether it's traditionally or independently published.

Preorders are considered the most important goal in marketing a new book. But getting those early orders can be challenging. You're asking consumers to get excited enough about your book to part with their money long before they can get their hands on it.

It can be done. Here are some techniques:

- Create 'buzz' by trumpeting the announcement of the book's title. If you're traditionally published, you can make a big deal out of this when you announce your book deal.
- Post a cover reveal.
- Write a great book description. Even traditional publishers reach out to the author to write or approve the back blurb.
- Reviews and quotes from other authors often catch readers' attention.
- Build a great website (if you don't already have it) and include a subscription form on your website asking for visitors' email addresses.
- Build an author's street team. A street team is a group of fans that volunteer to promote you. Collaborators have double the chance for obvious reasons. Unless you're hermits like us and have your heads buried in the sand.
- Test and improve your book cover and description. Our Nik James publisher is an avid believer in this process. They have already changed the covers of our upcoming publications based on audience test responses.
- Create swag, especially if it ties in to the story in some way. And keep in mind that your name on a tag on a water bottle probably gets thrown away. But your cover on a coffee mug lasts much longer.
- Release an 'exclusive preview' excerpt on your website or on a blog post or in a newsletter.
- Give away Advance Reading Copies to drive early reviews.

- Create 'countdown' social media posts.
- Use paid subscription services like BookBub to announce the preorder.

The list above is certainly not all-inclusive. But think of it as a starting point as you collaborate on a plan.

Publication
Or, The Book Birthday

Let's move on to the launch day, or as many writers like to call it, the 'book birthday'.

We'll cover some old ways (radio interviews, national media, print publications) and newer ways that can be used to promote a brand new release. Traditional publishers have a firm hold on many of the old ways of promoting an author's work. But that doesn't mean the independent writing team cannot still benefit from knowing and pursuing some of these strategies.

The Press Release

A press release seems really old fashioned, but it's still an important way of letting the media know what's new with you. So how do we write one?

- Write it like a newspaper story.
- Put a 'hook' into the first paragraph (the lead).
- Keep the lead under 35 words.
- Start with the most important information in the lead and then work your way down.
- Answer the 5 W's: Who, What, Where, When, Why.

- Use short sentences and short paragraphs. Try not to use more than three sentences per paragraph.
- Write in simple, tight, concise language.
- Keep it short. Do it in letter form.
- Be sure to include a contact name and phone number and email address so it will be easy for a reporter to contact you.

We send the press release via email to local and regional news outlets. The secret is to make the news editor's job easy by providing usable material to fill those columns. There are dozens of websites that give examples online.

The Video Book Trailer

Joanna Penn of *The Creative Penn* sees five obvious benefits of book trailers:

1. Videos are popular.
2. They are easy to share.
3. They help the reader get to know you.
4. They keep your book fresh in the reader's head.
5. They can be easy to make and don't require further investment.

Book Tours

In the past, book tours were events which typically consisted of stopping in at bookstores or libraries or media outlets for readings and Q&A sessions. They were an immediate way of connecting to people who, amazingly, had decided to spend time with us and our work.

Because we were a collaborative writing team, the book was often forgotten, and the audience's interest shifted to wanting to know how we worked together. Having gone through this so many times, we were always prepared to talk on the topic at any time and never needed to stick to a script.

The recent pandemic pushed book tours to become virtual tours.

Claire Kirch stated in a recent article in *Publisher's Weekly*, "Pros and Cons of Virtual Events Weighed by Publishers and Booksellers":

> While the publishers' reps agreed that virtual events are effective in drawing large audiences from far beyond the bookstore's physical location, there are flip sides to virtual events ranging from the need to make each event on an author's tour unique to delivering a program that keeps viewers engaged.

You and your partner do offer something different, if not unique. And your experience of working with one another will definitely keep viewers engaged.

Blog Tours

A blog tour is where you take your book on a virtual tour, hosted by various book blogs across the Internet. Book blogs are dedicated to books, writing, and related topics. You write the post that the blogger's readership will enjoy, and the owner of the site helps to promote your book.

A number of companies can be found online who will arrange blog tours for authors for a fee. But as far as how effective they are, opinions vary. And of course, all blog sites are not equal in their reach.

Book Promotion Newsletters

Book promotion newsletters are a dynamic component of the overall book industry and should be part of any marketing plan. The newsletters are great for readers, providing engagement with authors and news of upcoming releases. In addition to being free to readers, newsletters generally include offers of bargains, and everybody loves a bargain.

But for writers, be cautious. Some of these newsletters can work well; some are a waste of your precious time and money. Do your research.

Author Newsletter Email Blasts

On a regular basis and prior to the release of each new book, we email our newsletters to bookstores and fans that are on our mailing list. It's a hugely effective method of promotion. It may not work for everyone, but it works for us.

Readers love to feel that they are getting a glimpse into the writer's life. The email isn't just good at bringing you new readers, it's a tremendously good way of deepening your personal engagement with your audience.

Reviews

In the not-so-distant past, bookstore owners knew their regular customers and actively hand sold books they liked and felt were compatible with each reader's taste. Now, online reviews serve that purpose.

One thing we'd really stress – before and immediately after a book goes on sale, you want to get as many reviews posted online as possible. This is so important now that the number of brick-and-mortar bookstores is shrinking.

Most of the authors who seem to reside on the best-seller lists year after year have made it there by building a loyal readership over the course of many years prior to hitting the lists. Readers tell other readers, a reputation begins to build, and sales increase exponentially. Yes, readers buy books of authors that they trust will produce 'good reads.'

There may be no other industry out there where word-of-mouth matters as much as in publishing. It's important at every stage of the publishing business. So the number of books we write and the frequency of their release matters a lot.

The Black Hole

AKA, everything that we haven't mentioned.

Podcasts, live feeds on Instagram, Facebook parties, TikTok influencers, Snapchat, a blog of your own, getting involved with other writers' giveaways, paying publicists to advertise and generate buzz. There are so many possibilities out there.

If we consider the return on investment, online promotion offers an ever-changing world of opportunities for writers, opportunities none of us can afford to miss.

One important point that we need to mention here pertains to expectations. No matter how much money we are willing to spend on publicity or advertising or how many hours we spend on it, lasting success in this business comes over time. An ad campaign you are doing right now for your book might not bear fruit right away. It might take two or three books, or more, before you begin to build that valuable name recognition.

There are so many facets to promotion. We know we've barely scratched the surface. However, if we – as collaborative writers – harness the same creative synergy in this area as we do in our fiction writing, we can make a name for ourselves and sell books for a very long time.

That's it. Promotion can work.

The first priority, of course, is for the two of you to write the best book that you can. Then, go out and promote it together the way it deserves to be promoted. After all, writing and promotion are practically the only two things that you can truly control in this career you have chosen.

And the rest of it? Well, just celebrate with that partner of yours when the good times roll.

Afterword

The Family Reunion
or, Getting The Last Word In

In writing this book, we searched out the combined wisdom of a large number of writing teams so that more writers can find a way of experiencing the joys of collaborative writing – avoiding the pitfalls and working in harmony to produce quality fiction for a large number of readers.

We put this book together as a way of sharing an experience that we ourselves have found both fulfilling and rewarding on a number of levels. Collaboration provides an adventure in art and in relationships that we hope more people can experience, as well.

With the rapidly changing world of technology and publishing, however, we know that this book will not provide the final word on writing as we roll on into the future. That final word will come from writers like you. Perhaps in future editions of this book, we'll be able to include your experiences and wisdom.

Visit us on our website (www.MayMcGoldrick.com). We'll look forward to hearing from you ... and to reading those stories that you and your partners will be publishing in the years to come.

Nikoo and Jim McGoldrick

AKA:
   May McGoldrick (www.MayMcGoldrick.com)
   Jan Coffey (www.JanCoffey.com)
   Nik James (www.NikJamesAuthor.com)

Email us at: NikooandJim@gmail.com

About the Author

USA Today Bestselling Authors Nikoo and Jim McGoldrick have crafted over fifty fast-paced, conflict-filled contemporary and historical novels, along with two works of nonfiction, under the pseudonyms Jan Coffey, May McGoldrick, and Nik James.

These popular and prolific authors write suspense, mystery, American Westerns, historical romance, and young adult novels. They are four-time Rita Award Finalists and the winners of numerous awards for their writing, including the Daphne DeMaurier Award for Excellence, the *Romantic Times Magazine* Reviewers' Choice Award, three NJRW Golden Leaf Awards, two Holt Medallions, and the Connecticut Press Club Award for Best Fiction. Their work is included in the Popular Culture Library collection of the National Museum of Scotland.

Associated Writing Programs (AWP)

https://www.awpwriter.org/

A non-profit association working for the benefit of writers, writing programs, and teachers of writing. Articles and news, conference information, and job information.

Authorlink!

http://www.authorlink.com/

An award-winning news, information, and marketing service for editors, literary agents, and writers.

Authors Guild

http://www.authorsguild.org/

The Authors Guild, the nation's largest society of published authors, is an advocate for fair compensation, free speech, and copyright protection.

Horror Writers Association

http://www.horror.org

For writers in the fields of horror, the occult, and dark

fantasy. HWA currently has over 600 members, ranging from unpublished beginners up to Stephen King. Providing members with advice, networking, moral support, and other services.

International Women's Writing Guild

http://www.iwwg.com

The International Women's Writing Guild is a network for the personal and professional empowerment of women through writing.

Mystery Writers of America

https://mysterywriters.org/

Promoting and protecting the interests and welfare of mystery writers.

National Writers Union

http://www.nwu.org

The National Writers Union (UAW-AFL-CIO) is the trade union for freelance writers of all genres (journalism, books, poetry, technical, business, instructional, electronic). Committed to improving the economic and working conditions of freelance writers through the collective strength of their members. Offering member education, job banks, and much, much more.

Novelists, Inc.

http://www.ninc.com/

A coalition of working writers dedicated to serving the professional needs of its members. The site includes their newsletter, some helpful articles relating to various aspects of the writing life, and a list of books written by members. There is also a members only area.

Poets and Writers

http://www.pw.org

A nonprofit service organization for poets, fiction writers, performance poets, and writers of literary nonfiction. Includes dozens of pages on getting published, copyrighting your work, and more. The site features a search engine to help writers locate the resources they need. "Speakeasy," a message forum, creates an open discussion space for writers.

Romance Writers of America

http://www.rwanational.com

An organization dedicated to promoting the interests of romance writers, published and unpublished, through education, networking, and public relations.

Science Fiction and Fantasy Writers of America, Inc.

http://www.sfwa.org/

A non-profit organization whose primary purpose is to help SF/F authors deal effectively with agents, editors, anthologists. The website includes information and articles of use to writers at all levels of experience.

ShawGuides: The Guide to Writers Conferences

http://www.shawguides.com/writing/

Contains sponsor listings and the Writers Conference Calendar contains upcoming programs.

Sisters in Crime

https://www.sistersincrime.org/

Combating discrimination against women in the mystery field, educating publishers and the general public as to inequities in the treatment of female authors, raising awareness of their contribution to the field, and promoting the professional advancement of women who write mysteries.

Society of Children's Book Writers and Illustrators

http://www.scbwi.org

Offering information about the children's publishing industry and the organization to non-members.

Western Writers of America

https://westernwriters.org/

Promoting the literature of the American West and recognizing the best in Western writing. The organization membership includes fiction writers, historians and other nonfiction authors, young adult and romance writers, and writers interested in regional history.

Writers Write

http://www.writerswrite.com

A one-stop resource for professional writers. Offers a particularly good list of Writers' Associations and Organizations.

Bibliography

"Behind the Scenes with Judith Michael." Online. http://www.randomhouse.com/judithmichael/behind.html (27 February 1999).

"The Benefits of Collaboration." *Poets & Writers*. Online. http://www.pw.org/rw/caboc.htm (4 March 1999).

Bennett, Hal Zina and Michael Larsen. *How to Write with a Collaborator.* Cincinnati: Writer's Digest, 1988.

Berland, Nancy. "Hiring a Personal Publicist – The Whys, Wherefores and What It takes." *Romance Writers' Report* 19.3 (March 1999): 20-22.

Chase, Elaine Raco. "I Love Me-Who Does My Publisher Love? Or Should I do Publicity On My Own?" *Novelists' Ink.* 9.7 (July 1998): 1+.

Copeland, Hal. "How to Market Your Novel: A Publicist's Perspective." *Novelists' Ink.* Volume 9.7 (July 1998): 9-11.

Finch, Diana. "Minutes for the General Meeting." Association of Authors' Representatives (AAR). March 4, 1992.

Fortune, Beverly. "Author Indulges Youngsters' Fantasies." Online.
http://vh1383.infi.net/herald-leader/news/0130/fteach.html (28 February 1999).

Fournies, Ferdinand F. *Coaching for Improved Work Performance.* New York: Van Nostrand Reinhold, 1978.

Gray, John. *Men Are From Mars, Women Are From Venus.* New York: Harper Collins Publishers, 1992.

Lewis, Hunter. *A Question of Values: Six Ways We Make the Personal Choices That Shape Our Life.* San Francisco: Harper & Row, 1990.

Maass, Donald. *The Career Novelist.* Portsmouth: Heinemann, 1996.

Marshall, Edward M. *Transforming the Way We Work.* NY: AMACOM, 1995.

Maslow, Abraham H. *Motivation and Personality.* NY: Harper & Row, 1954.

Scarbrough, Marsha. "It Takes Two: The Write Relationship." Online.
http://www.wga.org/journal/1998/0498/dynamicduos.html (18 May 1998).

Skolnik, Peter. "Collaboration Agreement Checklist." Addendum to "Minutes for the General Meeting." Association of Authors' Representatives (AAR). March 4, 1992.

Snead, G. Lynne and Joyce Wycoff. *To Do...Doing...Done!* NY: Simon and Schuster, 1997.

Wilson, Edmund. *The Devils and Canon Barham: Ten Essays on Poets, Novelists and Monsters.* NY: Farrar, Straus and Giroux, 1968.

List of Contributing Teams

A number of writers who contributed to the 1st edition of *Marriage of Minds* have since passed on. Their talents and their knowledge and their willingness to share will be missed.

Lisa Barnett collaborated on three works of fiction with her partner Melissa Scott. Their first work, *The Armor of Light* was recently re-released (Baen Books, 1988 and NESFA Press, 1997). Her other works include *Point of Hopes* (Tor, 1995) and *Point of Dreams* (Tor, 2000). Lisa also worked as an editor and lived in New Hampshire with her partner of over twenty years.

Edo van Belkom is the author of over 200 stories of science fiction, fantasy, horror and mystery. In addition to winning the 1997 Bram Stoker Award from the Horror Writers Association for "Rat Food" (co-authored with David Nickle), his stories have twice been nominated for both the Aurora Award and the Arthur Ellis Award. His first novel, *Wyrm Wolf*, published in 1995, was a Locus bestseller and a finalist for the 1995 First Novel Bram Stoker Award. Other novels include *Lord Soth*, and *Mister Magick*. He has written nonfiction, *Northern Dreamers: Interviews with Famous Authors of Science Fiction, Fantasy and Horror* (Quarry Press, 1998), and a short story collection, *Death Drives a Semi* (Quarry Press, 1998). Edo lives in Brampton, Ontario, with his wife Roberta and son Luke.

Dixie Browning and Mary Williams (AKA Bronwyn Williams) are sisters who live on North Carolina's Outer Banks. They both have children, grandchildren, and retired husbands. Dixie has written sixty-seven contemporary romances for Silhouette under her own name and two (as Zoe Dozier) for Thomas Bouregy's Avalon line. More than forty of those were published before teaming up with her sister. As Bronwyn Williams, they've written a dozen historical romances and two novellas for Harlequin Historicals and Penguin Putnam.

Beth Ciotta and Cynthia Serra (AKA C.B. Scott), have collaborated on two paranormal romance novels. Working individually, Cynthia has written a children's book about a cockroach obsessed with Hawaiian Punch, and Beth has produced award-winning novels in a numerous genres, including paranormal, historical, contemporary, and steampunk romance.

Louie Dillon and JB Hamilton Queen are sisters and native Kentuckians. They share the same interests, and have worked together most of their lives, appearing in television commercials and working in the entertainment field. They completed three novels together. JB had a short story published in the October 1998 issue of *The Kentucky Explorer* and has gone on to publish six award-winning novels.

Kathryn Falk, Lady of Barrow. In the words of *The New York Times*, Kathryn Falk is the "Queen of Romance." She is the founder and publisher of *Romantic Times Magazine*, the bible of the romance industry. Starting the magazine in 1981 in a walk-in closet, she has taken *RT* from a newsletter to a 120-page glossy format that serves as a leading resource for writers, both established and aspiring, and for romance readers. She is the author of *How to Write A Romance and Get it Published*.

Shirl Henke and Carol Reynard (AKA Shirl Henke) are the award-winning and bestselling authors of twenty three novels. After a career in university teaching, Shirl Henke became a full-time romance writer. Carol Reynard contributes story, dialogue, research, and translates Shirl's illegible scrawl into the computer.

Amy Ingram of Silver Spring, Maryland, is a career journalist and writer. Amy's work has been published in numerous magazines and newspapers on a variety of topics. *Harvest of the Heart* was her first collaborative historical romance novel.

Lori and Tony Karayianni (AKA Tori Carrington) Collaborative writers as well as life partners, this husband and wife team penned over fifty novels together for Harlequin Temptation before Tony's passing.

Lynn Kerstan, formerly a college teacher and professional bridge player, was the award-winning author of over a dozen novels and novellas set in early 19th-century England. Lynn's collaboration with Alicia Rasley involved one novel, *Gwen's Christmas Ghost*. This novel went on to win 1996 RITA award for Best Regency Romance.

Deborah Mazoyer and Shelley Mosley (AKA Deborah Shelley) have written three novels for Kensington Publishers. Deborah is an architect whose prior writing experience consisted of construction and building code brochures, and technical reports. Shelley is a Library Manager and began publishing her poems and stories when she was eight years old. Shelley has also written a newspaper column, satirical lyrics, and over 600 limericks – one of which won first place in an *Affaire de Coeur Magazine* contest.

Leslie-Christine Megahey & Shirley Holden-Ferdinand (AKA Christine Holden) are a mother-daughter writing team who have been working together since 1991. Shirley has been writing since she was 16, and Leslie penned her first story at the age of 4, a school project that sits proudly on the shelf at home. They published five novels together, and Leslie continues to write as Leslie C. Ferdinand.

David Nickle is a reporter for a chain of community newspapers in Toronto, Canada, where he writes about city council. He is also an author of fifteen published works of short fiction, and co-author of the novel *The Claus Effect* (with Karl Schroeder). In 1998, he was co-recipient of the Bram Stoker Award for Superior Achievement in short fiction for another collaboration, "Rat Food" (with Edo Van Belkom). David has had one of his stories adapted as an episode in the Showtime series *The Hunger*.

Cynthia Oberle has been writing since she was in kindergarten and dreamed of being an author. For a time in high school, she quit writing and took up acting... which is why she believes her writing is so melodramatic at times. Thanks to her writing partner and best friend, Cynthia found her way back to writing. She and her partner collaborated on one novel, *Harvest of the Heart*.

Bernice P. Picard and Lee Rouland collaborate on children's fantasy novels and adult mysteries. Bernice is a mother, grandmother, and an avid golfer. Individually, she has written science fiction novels and is a member of Romance Writers of America and Mystery Writers of America. Lee has a degree in psychology so it follows that she's been a printer's assistant, a school teacher, a blueberry picker, a payroll administrator, an astrologer, and a webmaster. On her own, Lee is the author of two short fantasy pieces in addition to the mystery short story, "Car Trouble," which was optioned for television. She and her husband live in southern New Jersey, pretending it's France.

Alicia Rasley is the award-winning author of Regency period novels. Alicia worked for eight years at two Indiana colleges, which taught her that she prefers leading workshops for fiction writers to teaching freshman composition! She now teaches classes online and in workshops around the country. She has penned numerous books on writing and collaborated on one book with Lynn Kerstan, *Gwen's Christmas Ghost*, which won the 1996 RITA award for Best Regency Romance.

Melissa Scott wrote three novels with her partner, Lisa Barnett, and over two dozen novels solo. Her work in science fiction and fantasy has earned her numerous awards, including the John W. Campbell Award for Best New Writer, and the Lambda Award in both 1995 and 1996. She is also the author of *Conceiving the Heavens:*

Creating the Science Fiction Novel. Melissa has a Ph.D. in history from Brandeis University.

Lea Tassie, a former real estate sales person and flight attendant, is now chartered accountant. Lea has published poems, articles, and short stories, and she is also the co-author of the nonfiction book, *Humour Is The Best Sauce.* In addition to writing full-time on her own, Lea collaborated on a suspense novel, *Ashes,* with Kathleen Webb. She presently lives in Victoria B.C. with her husband, a former journalist, and an imperious black and white cat called Whiskey.

Kathleen Webb believes she is a blend of wordsmith and storyteller, happy writing both fiction and nonfiction. Kathleen's first national sale was to *Cosmopolitan* magazine and has since published in a variety of periodicals both in Canada and the US. In her own words, she is a sucker for a happy ending and thus has always been drawn to the world of romance fiction. She bought her first training bra and her first Harlequin around the same time. To date, she has published eight romance novels.

CPSIA information can be obtained
at www.ICGtesting.com
Printed in the USA
BVHW080556040321
601655BV00004B/155